P9-ECN-740

WITHDRAWN

POINT LOMA NAZARENE UNIVERSITY
RYAN LIBRARY
3900 LOMALAND DRIVE
SAN DIEGO, CALIFORNIA 92106-2899

The Contributors

Earl L. Avery, Special Assistant to the President, Bentley College

Darlyne Bailey, Dean and Associate Professor, Mandel School of Applied Social Sciences, Case Western Reserve University

Myrtle P. Bell, University of Texas–Arlington

Bonita L. Betters-Reed, Professor of Management, Simmons College

David M. Boje, Head of the Department of Management, College of Business Administration and Economics, New Mexico State University

Linda McGee Calvert, Consultant

Cliff Cheng, University of Southern California

Dina Comnenou, Associate Professor, Lesley College

Peter Couch, Professor of Management, Illinois State University

Marcy Crary, Associate Professor of Management, Bentley College

M. Colleen Jones, Assistant Professor of Management, University of Nebraska–Lincoln

Gordon W. Meyer, Associate Professor, Canisius College

Lynda L. Moore, Associate Professor of Management, Simmons College

Duncan Spelman, Associate Professor, Bentley College

Barbara A. Walker, Consultant

Teaching Diversity

Joan V. Gallos
V. Jean Ramsey
and Associates

658.3041
G173t
4/99

Teaching Diversity

Listening to the Soul, Speaking from the Heart

POINT LOMA NAZARENE UNIVERSITY
WITHDRAWN
RYAN LIBRARY

Jossey-Bass Publishers
San Francisco

Copyright © 1997 Jossey-Bass Inc., Publishers, 350 Sansome Street, San Francisco, California 94104.

All rights reserved. No part of this publication may be reproduced, stored in a retrieval system, or transmitted, in any form or by any means, electronic, mechanical, photocopying, recording, or otherwise, without the prior written permission of the publisher.

Substantial discounts on bulk quantities of Jossey-Bass books are available to corporations, professional associations, and other organizations. For details and discount information, contact the special sales department at Jossey-Bass Inc., Publishers (415) 433–1740; Fax (800) 605–2665.

For sales outside the United States, please contact your local Simon & Schuster International Office.

 Manufactured in the United States of America on Lyons Falls Pathfinder Tradebook. This paper is acid-free and 100 percent totally chlorine-free.

Library of Congress Cataloging-in-Publication Data

Gallos, Joan V.
    Teaching diversity : listening to the soul, speaking from the
heart / Joan V. Gallos, V. Jean Ramsey and associates.
       p.   cm. — (The Jossey-Bass business & management series)
(The Jossey-Bass higher & adult education series)
    Includes bibliographical references and index.
    ISBN 0-7879-0325-6
    1. Diversity in the workplace—Study and teaching.   I. Ramsey,
V. Jean. II. Title. III. Series. IV. Series: Jossey-Bass higher
and adult education series.
HF5549.5.M5G35 1997
658.3′1244—dc20   96-32707

FIRST EDITION
HB Printing   10 9 8 7 6 5 4 3 2 1

A joint publication in
The Jossey-Bass Business & Management Series
and
The Jossey-Bass Higher & Adult Education Series

Contents

Preface

Teaching workplace diversity is increasingly essential and increasingly complex. Demographers paint technicolor and multicultural portraits of the U.S. workforce in the twenty-first century, and our everyday work experiences support their predictions. Recognizing the bottom-line implications of the changing nature of the workforce, organizations of all kinds are scrambling to explore what it means for their structures, policies, practices, and training efforts. Universities question how well their programs prepare tomorrow's leaders to manage a diverse workforce.

Spurred by organizational needs and guidelines from accrediting agencies like the American Association of Collegiate Schools of Business, colleges and universities are struggling with the question of how best to integrate diversity issues into curricula and programs. Their responses vary from limited coverage at the discretion of the instructor to clear requirements for all students to take a course emphasizing diversity before graduation. At the same time, corporate educators, unable to draw from time- and market-tested programs and strategies, are working to develop their own forums and models for learning about and responding to workplace diversity. Variety characterizes their efforts as well: activities range from optional diversity workshops to corporatewide strategic initiatives that permeate all aspects of company policy and life. Individual instructors and trainers, striving for relevance and consistency with institutional missions, face questions of how to teach well about this increasingly important topic. There seems little agreement on how best to prepare individuals for the challenges of a diverse workforce. There is even less agreement on how to prepare the educators who do this important work.

All evidence, however, points to the reality that teaching diversity effectively is difficult. It is different from other management education: it is more than teaching content or objectively describing a set of issues. Effective diversity education reaches to the core of instructor and students as both work together to probe a wide spectrum of social forces and personal issues. Diversity education questions our institutions and policies, values and behaviors, definitions of truth and equity, choices and omissions, self-images and professional roles. Not as simple as assigning a book or imparting information about new management techniques and skills, teaching diversity requires a deep personal journey of self-discovery and growth. It means learning to listen to the soul and speak from the heart.

Teaching Diversity explores the journey of diversity education. It offers guidance and support for anyone who may travel into the world of diversity teaching and training. It is written for management educators but is equally useful for all who seek insights and understandings about how to teach and learn more effectively about differences. Through a series of open explorations of the issues and gently guided interludes, it suggests ways to prepare for this complex teaching task and offers instructors and trainers a map to help them understand the diversity terrain, choose personal paths, recognize crossroads, compare alternative routes, anticipate roadblocks, sustain commitment, support fellow travelers, and celebrate the joys and benefits of the journey.

Content of the Book

This book brings together the voices of seventeen individuals currently engaged in diversity education. It offers a unique opportunity to look below the surface and behind the scenes at the diversity teaching and learning process. Not a standard edited text or a how-to manual, this book contains open and honest accounts from a diverse set of individuals. Contributors share personal and professional experiences and write with passion and openness not typically found in academic books. Interludes by the editing authors—guideposts along the way—focus themes and issues, identify paradoxes in the teaching-learning struggles, and probe more deeply the parallels in the individual experiences. The result, we believe, is a powerful exploration of previously unexamined issues—the emotional tension, personal growth, soul searching, intellectual excitement, professional satisfaction, complexity, setbacks, learning, unique preparation, opportunities, pain, and deep pleasure involved in educating sound leaders for a diverse work world.

This book is divided into five parts. Part One has three sections, devoted to the topics of identity, preparation, and the experience of being "othered." These sections examine the antecedents to diversity teaching, exploring critical experiences that lead to and shape one's perspective toward the work.

Part Two has four sections that explore the nature of diversity teaching itself—definition of the work, how it differs from other teaching and training, how diversity teaching evolves over time, and the choices educators make in their approaches to the work.

Part Three has seven sections that take readers behind the scenes to examine the uniqueness of the diversity teaching and learning process. These sections explore the teacher as learner; shifts in teacher-student roles and relationships; the personal and emotional nature of diversity education; institutional, structural, and systemic issues that affect teaching and learning; dilemmas and paradoxes inherent in the process; benefits from team teaching; and diversity education beyond classroom walls.

Part Four looks "inside" the diversity educator. Its three sections explore the vulnerability, pain and anger, and self-reflection that are regular features of the work.

Part Five examines the ways in which diversity educators keep themselves going. Four sections here explore sustaining commitment to the work, collaborating and community building, experiencing the joys and benefits of diversity teaching, and seeing a future for diversity education.

In a concluding chapter, we—the editing authors—offer reflections on the joys and complexities of diversity teaching. We explore the importance of a strong pedagogy of learning in diversity work, the foundation for and important contributions of diversity education, the critical need to become more multicultural, the central role of paradox in diversity work, the importance of preparation and faculty development, the essential need for community, and the future of diversity education. The book concludes with a rich listing of resources on diversity.

Purpose of the Book

We undertook this book project for multiple reasons. At a simple level, we wanted to fill a gap we saw in the workplace diversity literature. We searched for books that dug deeply into diversity teaching and learning issues—ones that addressed the needs of educators like us who prepare present and future managers for an increasingly diverse work world. We could not find one. We looked then for works that probed the interconnections among developmental, cognitive, and socioemotional issues for teachers and students in the classroom or training room. We drew a blank there as well. Accepting the challenge to do something about the situation, we conceptualized this book.

On a deeper level, we undertook this project with a clear purpose to influence diversity education. We wanted to make a difference in how people think about, prepare for, and carry out diversity teaching. We have been frustrated watching institutions and organizations continue to define this different and difficult educational work in traditional, hierarchical terms. Diversity education is not "teaching as usual." We have been pained watching the need for effective diversity education outstrip the supply of thoughtful materials, pedagogies, courses, and educators. Domestic and international events call loudly and clearly for more and very different learning about how to value and live productively with our differences. We have been saddened to see diversity educators struggling alone to understand the complexity of the work. Effective preparation and consistent support are sorely needed. We have been frightened by those who advocate social backlash and a return to "business as usual" and those who naively believe that the necessary diversity work has already been done. We felt compelled to take a stand—to advocate something different.

We believe that *Teaching Diversity* does that. It offers realistic insights into learning and teaching diversity. It dispels romantic notions about the task. It reminds diversity educators of the importance of engaging heart, soul, and mind in their work. It encourages a different kind of preparation for teaching—the need to push aside traditional educational notions, roll up one's sleeves, and dig into deep learning for all. It warns educators to expect different outcomes from their work—longer-term goals, deeper personal development, more powerful learning for teacher and student. It advocates going beyond the individual and the interpersonal in diversity education. Institutional, structural, and systemic issues are powerful and pervasive barriers to equity that cannot be ignored. It educates organizational decision makers about the unique requirements for successful diversity teaching efforts. It reminds all that diversity education is steeped in paradox, demanding abilities to value and live with contradictions.

Creation of the Book

The process by which this book was created is itself a lesson in diversity, illustrating what can happen when a diverse group of people get together in nontraditional and supportive ways. This project has been intentionally "different" from its inception, in process as well as content.

First, we wanted a diverse group of educators for this project. It seemed only natural for a book on diversity education to involve people from a wide variety of backgrounds with a range of experience and preparation. We looked for full-time university professors, as well as those who teach on a more ad hoc basis. We selected individuals who taught in states as geographically and culturally diverse as California, Ohio, Massachusetts, Illinois, Texas, New York, and Missouri. We involved educators who teach in small, private schools, as well as in large, public ones; in universities located in major cities, as well as those in more rural areas; in schools whose students are predominantly White, as well as one whose students are predominantly Black. We found contributors who are full-time consultants or administrators. We were delighted to involve diversity educators at a variety of career stages, from doctoral student to semiretiree.

The contributors are diverse on other dimensions as well. They are Euro-American, African-American, Chinese-American, and Greek-American. They are female and male and come from a wide range of socioeconomic backgrounds. Ages range from the mid-thirties to the mid-sixties. Contributors also differ in how they define their diversity work, the degree to which they see themselves engaged in it, their approaches to it, and the ways in which they carry out their strategies for change.

Beyond having a diverse set of contributors, it was also important to us to make the project developmental in the broadest sense of the word. We wanted opportunities for learning and growth for ourselves as well as for the contributors. We wanted to encourage a different kind of thinking and writing about the diversity teaching work we all do—to let our spirits soar and creativity speak in ways not often encouraged in traditional academic or corporate settings. We also wanted to develop a sense of community among a broadly diverse group of colleagues, some of whom knew each other well, others not. We knew this demanded open interactions, exchange, and something different from the normal anthology where individuals contribute discrete, separate chapters.

Perhaps most important, however, to us as editors and orchestrators of the project, we wanted it to be fun. This may not seem a significant developmental issue, but for the two of us, both intense compulsives with latent workaholic tendencies, there was much to learn (and relearn) if we were to work joyously, openly, and stress-free together. The project began in a playful and spontaneous manner with a late-night conversation in our shared dorm room during the 1994 Organizational Behavior Teaching Conference. We moved from possibility to proposal to contract with ease and speed. We wanted to maintain and cultivate that spirit and ease throughout the project. It had freed us to think in new ways. We hoped this would continue and spread to the contributors as well.

We didn't know exactly what this developmentally based book-writing process would be like. Our initial vision involved somehow weaving individual themes and voices together in a way that would benefit readers professionally but also touch them in personal and profound ways. Our intent was to create a rich tapestry of shared and collective experiences, providing insight and guidance to others who embark on their own diversity teaching and learning journeys. We had vague images of common themes surfacing from what contributors chose to explore and our own ideas about what we wanted educators to examine. We knew we'd need to remain open and flexible. We wanted the magic of discovery somehow wedded with the clarity and organization necessary for real learning.

To do all this, we needed individuals willing to listen to their souls, find their "voices," and speak from the heart in ways not asked for elsewhere. It was important that contributors be willing to set aside academic ways of writing and engage instead in what we called "free-flowing, colorful, emotionally charged, and personal" writing. We didn't want people who had the whole thing figured out (if indeed they exist). We tapped diversity educators whom we knew struggled with the issues—people themselves on a developmental path of discovery who would welcome an opportunity to speak openly and honestly about their experiences.

We also knew that all this could work only with individuals we trusted and felt would trust us enough to accept the initial ambiguity of the project. After all, we were asking professional educators to open their hearts and souls, knowing that we were likely to respond to their contributions with more than the usual "revise and resubmit." We planned to push and probe, suggest and request, cut and paste. We warned people that we might, for example, come across a sentence of critical importance to the book, go back to them, and ask them to develop that one sentence into a freestanding submission. We gave no guarantees regarding how much of what people wrote would be published, nor did we offer much clarity about the form in which their words might appear. Our vision of community, mutuality, and feminine wholeness asked contributors to make a much larger commitment than usually required for an edited book. In retrospect, it is a miracle that almost everyone we approached signed on with gusto.

The process of creating this book was an ongoing, iterative one—between the contributors and the editing authors, among the contributors, and between the editing authors. We are grateful to all for their flexibility, trust, and willingness to write and rewrite only to have wonderful writing land on the cutting room floor. The friendship, fun, and community we envisioned became a reality. The process was truly one of creation, discovery, and learning. The interactions have been full of support and encouragement, valuable feedback, and learning.

From the moment the first drafts arrived, it was clear that we had something powerful. Multiple voices—different in style, tone, and detail—spoke to common issues. Our initial intuition about the form of the book seemed confirmed: the most effective way of presenting the "stories" of these diversity educators was to pull the larger manuscripts apart and weave them into a polyphonic whole. The diversity in the voices was as great as the diversity in the messages. The juxtaposition of the two made both even more compelling.

This is no ordinary volume of edited pieces. It is a jointly created book that captures the experiences and expertise of all. As editors, we provided the overall framework of a journey metaphor that was influenced and shaped in profound and varied ways by the contributors. Our questions, comments, suggestions, and editorial work influenced contributors' submissions in direction and scope. In turn, the content of submissions and free-flowing exchanges with contributors helped us identify critical issues. Interactions continued. Community strengthened. We wrote our own contributions from the heart. We worked as grand weavers with the writing of others—capturing themes, weaving together separate strands into pleasing, comfortable, and at times provocative patterns. We offered interludes and bridges, suggestions, and next steps.

We also lived up to our promise to enjoy the project and have fun. The book conceived in a dorm room in a late-night talk session reminiscent of a teenage pajama party was further elaborated on warm spring days in Joan's backyard in Kansas City. Our best work, however, was done in the mountains of Santa Fe. We are convinced that the quality of the final book owes much to the peace and spiritual presence of the mountains—as well as to the green chile, Native American jewelry, and fetishes we also found there.

It seems only right that the work of two editing authors on the topic of diversity should be "diversity in action." We found this to be the case. As the project unfolded, one of us was more often comfortable brainstorming ideas, writing enthusiastically, going with the flow of the creative energy; the other, more comfortable cutting and pasting, weaving seemingly disparate pieces together, and managing the myriad administrative details in a project that involved seventeen individuals. When we met, invariably one of us would do most of the talking, the other, most of the note taking. One would be full of enthusiasm—the "we can do it" spirit—about the time the other's energy would flag. One could envision it all coming together while the other was convinced it would end in an incomprehensible mishmash. One would argue vehemently for inclusion of a certain point; the other would yield gracefully. One would find quiet, reflective moments to devote to the project while the other was "snowed under" with competing demands.

Our roles shifted dramatically throughout; the magic seemed to be in our natural complementarity. One who had been calm would panic in the face of unattended demands, just about the time that the overwhelmed other would find new space in her life for the project. One would be filled with hope and direction at the time the other was ready to throw in the towel. And so it went for two years. For both of us, the book became a good friend and provided solace in the midst of busy and challenging lives. Our work spaces became rooms filled with the voices of esteemed diversity educators, speaking from the heart about important and thought-provoking issues. We became connected to the contributors and each other in ways that surprised and delighted us.

Despite the distance between Kansas City and Houston, we were able to complete the book project for several reasons. The most important was probably our trust in, respect for, and willingness to yield to the sacred nature of the work. Despite our differences, we shared a commitment to the importance of the task and to the creation of growth-filled ways to do the work. We both wanted to stretch ourselves and others. We wanted to engage more than the intellect. We wanted to offer readers opportunity to do the same. We acknowledged the unique strengths we each brought to the project but also knew that we were part of something that was meant to be. Things came too easily, worked out too well, despite what on the surface might have seemed insurmountable odds. We kept waiting for it to overwhelm us; instead, magical moments multiplied. We learned through all this that sacred work and important contributions to knowledge don't have to be stress-filled. Like diversity teaching and learning, listening to and following one's heart is satisfying to body and soul.

August 1996   Joan V. Gallos
                                                 Kansas City, Missouri

                                                 V. Jean Ramsey
                                                 Houston, Texas

Acknowledgments

Book writing is tough business. We feel fortunate to have been supported, encouraged, and nurtured throughout this project by many people who deserve our thanks, love, and appreciation.

Thanks go first to the contributors in this volume for their openness, powerful stories, encouragement, and willingness to work enthusiastically and collaboratively with us. They have taught us much about diversity education and a learning community. It has been a delight to work closely with such good friends and colleagues. Many of these bonds are ongoing, and others were renewed during the project. New relationships were developed as a result of the work together. We thank each contributor and publicly express our deep affection and respect.

We also express our appreciation to Bill Hicks, now publisher of New Lexington Press, for his initial encouragement of this project. Bill brought us to Jossey-Bass, worked with us during the initial phases of the project, and gave us a combination of wise guidance and wide leeway to develop a creative, nontraditional edited work. We thank him for his trust and friendship.

A sincere thank-you goes to Byron Schneider at Jossey-Bass, who inherited in midstream two strong-willed women and a project with a life of its own. Byron's helpful feedback and respectful attention to detail and quality have enriched this work.

Research and book writing take time and resources. A special thank-you to Dean Young Pai and Associate Dean Linda Edwards at the University of Missouri–Kansas City School of Education and to Priscilla Slade, dean of the Jesse H. Jones School of Business at Texas Southern University, for their unfailing support and interest in this project. Jean is most grateful to John H. Williams, assistant dean, colleague, and friend, for his quiet but persistent ability to "run interference" for her. This book owes much to the many ways in which he protected her from others' ideas of how she might spend her time.

Administrative details are endless in a project of this scope. We thank Joan's graduate assistant, Sharadaprasad H. Ramadevanahalli, who provided computer wizardry and other assistance at critical junctures. Her secretary, Betty Green, brought her inimitable style and organization to her work for the book. Victoria Ndubuisi, while not working directly on the book, freed Jean's time by quietly, competently, and always cheerfully picking up the slack on other administrative responsibilities. Bobbie Richardson, too, and the dean's staff, Georgia Houston and Erika Vallier, helped keep Jean sane amid the seemingly endless bureaucratic maze of daily life in a university. Tony Hammond did a marvelous job of looking after her computer needs.

Our colleagues in the School of Business at Texas Southern University, the School of Education at the University of Missouri–Kansas City, and elsewhere deserve credit for their unfailing patience and good humor over the past two years. They have endured, we are sure, too many stories about this project and lived with the implications of our exhaustion and complete preoccupation with book writing. We send special thanks to Doug Toma, Dick Palm, Ed Underwood, Ralph Parish, Eugene Eubanks, B. J. Confer, Cindy Pemberton, Nancy Murdock, John George, Vena Long, Vicki Barham, Tony Manzo, Brenda Fasken, Dianne Smith, Stuart McAninch, Clara Wiley, Luzine Bickham, Joe Haley, Jean Latting, Stephanie Foy, and Forrest Aven. Joan also thanks her teachers and mentors, especially Chris Argyris, Don Schön, Fritz Steele, and John Van Maanen, whose models of good teaching, perspectives on pedagogy, and commitments to deep learning have stayed with her for more than twenty years. Jean acknowledges Kathy Kaplan for modeling the magic of a project like this—the freedom to be creative, intellectually fluid, heartfelt, and soulful.

We also owe a huge debt to the students in our classes, present and past. They have taught us much about teaching, learning, and valuing diversity; have listened to more than their fair share of book stories and examples; and have served as constant reminders of what this project is really all about.

The Organizational Behavior Teaching Society (OBTS) deserves some credit for the conception of this project. The focus on teaching and the playful spirit of its annual conference fed our creativity and led to our initial launching of this enterprise. Our overlapping terms on the OBTS board of directors helped us identify our commonalities and shared interests in learning and issues of equity.

Friends are an important part of sustaining commitment to book writing. We were fortunate that many of our friends were part of this project. Others were there to urge us onward at critical crossroads and moments of possible despair. Sandy Renz, Terry Deal, Peter Frost, Amy and Michael Sales, Rochelle and Steven Seltzer, Tom King, and Dale Fitzgibbons all deserve mention. A special note of appreciation goes to colleagues and friends Ella Bell and Stella Nkomo for taking time from their own book writing to read and comment on an earlier draft of our work.

We are not alone in having many to thank. The contributors acknowledge Carole Thomas, Nathaniel H. Mayes, Amber L. Mayes, Donald C. McNeil, Charles C. D. Hamilton, Grace Ann Rosile, Nora King, Charles Z. Wilson, Nickerson Garden residents, Dan Gilbert, Janet Gillespie, Pat Meyer, Iris Perkins, Earnest Bell, Toni King, Bob Dennehy, Willie Mae Thompson, Richard Thompson, Patricia Bell-Scott, Philip Hubbard, Philip Jones, Jerry Harvey, Peter Vaill, Erik Winslow, Ella Bell, Stella Nkomo, Abdelmagid Mazen, Iris Bailey, Arthur Bailey, and Sharon Y. Robinson for their diverse gifts and significant contributions to the life stories shared in this volume.

We have saved our strongest thanks for last. We thank our families and close friends for their love, support, and affection in the face of our compulsive book writing and work styles. They encourage and support us in our work even when it means spending time away from them. They value us for who we are. We feel blessed.

Joan sends a special thank-you to her sons, Christopher and Bradley Bolman. Parenting these two loving and creative free spirits has taught her much about teaching and learning, appreciating differences, and remaining humble. Bradley's empathy, sweetness, and persistent interest in his mother's work—"How was your day? Is the book finished yet?"—are more than a mother could ask from a son who has lived half his life with this project in the background. Chris, author of four novels by age eleven, accepted with grace his mother's absence at basketball and soccer games, logged in long hours entertaining his younger brother, and offered "author to author" support at critical times in the project. Thanks, guys. I love you.

Joan acknowledges, with affection, the encouragement of her father, John Gallos, who, despite his increasing frailty, never lost interest in this project. His final act of love and support was to hang tenaciously on to life until the first draft of the book was completed. His death in January 1996 was a profound loss, but his spirit and love of learning live on. We know he would have been proud to see this work in print.

Finally, Joan thanks her husband and closest colleague, Lee Bolman. Their friendship of twenty years has been marked by collaboration, love, intellectual challenge, support for individual differences, deep affection, and more than a few wild developmental adventures. Lee provided valuable feedback on the first draft of the manuscript and took on the lion's share of the basketball and soccer games, dinners, school pickups, and milk runs during this project. For all you do, Lee, this one's for you.

Jean particularly thanks her sons and daughter for their continued love and steadfast belief in who she is and what she stands for and for their patience with her not always having the time to share as much of their lives as she might like. Most important, though, she is grateful for their willingness to give her the freedom to continue to grow and develop. Never once has she heard them say "mothers/grandmothers/great-grandmothers shouldn't act that way!" Instead, they have allowed her to continue to evolve, not holding her to the "way things used to be." She also is grateful to Mel and Therese for what they bring to her son's lives and to Stephanie for "adopting" her new grandmother so quickly. And hugs and kisses to Kara, her granddaughter, and Johnny Lee, her great-grandson, for the constant surprises and delight they bring to all of our lives. They lovingly and innocently accept difference. They haven't yet been taught that it creates problems. We have much to learn from them.

Jean also is grateful to her brother, Dave, and his wife, Betty, and to her sisters, Nancy and Carol, for the time spent together in the past few years. It has been wonderful getting reacquainted in new ways, being reminded once more that we will always be there for one another, and that we share so many values as well as love for one another. Our mother would be (and was) very proud of us.

Finally, Jean feels especially blessed to have had her very special friend, Dave Barnes, come back into her life during this period. He has saved her from her "work self" on numerous occasions. He has shared his deck, his hopes and dreams, his free spirit, and his playfulness, as well as his ability to listen carefully and reflect deeply. He has taught her much about staying in the moment and living each day to its fullest.

All this love and support has created a wonderful space in which we did this work.

J.V.G.
V.J.R

Teaching Diversity

Part I

Starting Point for the Journey

Identity

*I*t seems appropriate to begin an exploration of the joys and challenges of teaching workplace diversity with the essential starting point for the journey: identity. For many diversity educators, who they are is intricately woven into their definition of the diversity teaching task. It affects their "take" on the issues. Values and beliefs, rooted in family histories and personal experiences, fuel the initial choice to do diversity teaching and sustain commitment to the work. For diversity educators, the personal is the professional, the professional is the personal—the two cannot be disentangled.

Teaching workplace diversity demands a different pedagogical stance and personal connection to the teaching task. As the stories of the contributors illustrate, it is identity-based and identity-driven work. In diversity teaching, the topic and teaching process are difficult to separate: "who I am" is the central focus of both.

All good teachers and trainers bring "who they are" to the educational arena: they attend to the intricacies of the moment, attune themselves to classroom interactions and relationships, work to stimulate thought and relevant questions, try to model active learning, and bring their own slant on topics and issues. They manage classroom dynamics and make choices for how to teach. Diversity teaching and training, however, demand even more.

Effective diversity educators know themselves and their roots well. They bring that knowledge openly and explicitly into their educational work, using themselves and their experiences to drive both how and what *they teach. A grounded identity and self-knowledge are gifts to be shared with others who seek to learn about similarities and differences. Respect for human differences comes easily for those who see valuing diversity as consistent with who they are.*

The identity stories that follow are tales of individual passion and commitment that often began early in life. The contributors trace the connections between their sense of identity and their diversity work and identify significant events that influenced their present involvement and concern.

In this section, you will meet all the educators who contribute their experiences and perspectives to this book. (In subsequent sections, not all voices speak on all issues.) All talk openly about themselves and their paths to diversity work. The wholeness—the integration of self and work so apparent in these stories—serves as a powerful reminder that diversity education is unique and challenging work.

Part of My Life
Earl Avery

It all began with the civil rights movement and my small role in several organizations in Los Angeles. As a college student, I was involved in the Student Nonviolent Coordinating Council (SNCC): I did things like sell T-shirts and sweatshirts to raise money for voter registration and had many discussions with roommates and friends about these issues. As an undergraduate, I also served as commissioner of community services and helped get more than five hundred college students involved in various community service programs. In addition, I worked with a group of classroom teachers—friends of mine—putting together a nonprofit organization to develop and disseminate materials on multicultural issues for elementary school kids in California.

Later I became a child advocate for the Massachusetts Child Advocacy Center. There I worked for children with special needs— kids who were thrown out of school or given no services. Cases ranged from students needing total residential programs to students of color arbitrarily put into special-needs classes or denied services. I saw a range of issues there: discovered how many children were not being served—how many kids of color were being mislabeled—and learned to intervene in school systems. In the civil rights movement, I did protests and so on; as a child advocate, I did different kinds of hands-on work that directly changed systems.

About eight years ago, I came to Bentley College as its affirmative action officer. I view my teaching at Bentley as another way of addressing issues going on in our society. To some of my teaching, I bring firsthand knowledge. I certainly came along at a time when overt discrimination was rampant in this country—I've been told, "You can't use that restroom." My father scored highest on a Civil Service exam in Los Angeles, for example, but rather than give him the job, they removed it. I grew up in communities other than housing projects; however, my family started out in a housing project that was a mix of Black and Hispanic. Up to the third grade, my next-door neighbor was a Chicano boy about my age. We spent a lot of time together. All of these experiences have contributed to my wanting to have an impact.

My being involved in diversity teaching work is tied to my history and what I'm all about. I can't envision a time in my life when talking about these issues and trying to address them, either directly or indirectly, will not be part of my life. It's not tied to money. It's not tied to my profession. It's tied to who I am.

A Continuing Story
Darlyne Bailey

The impact of, and my response to, the reality of multiplicity in the world has its seeds in the earliest years of my life. It continues to show itself in all aspects of who I am—an African-American woman, teacher-learner, researcher, administrator, daughter, sister, partner, aunt, niece, cousin, godchild, godmother, and friend who identifies as bisexual and experiences life as a divine blessing of magical interconnections. Here are highlights of my story.

I was born into a family that identifies as Negro yet embraced the other ethnicities that complete "us." I grew up in a town that actively supported the rights of all individuals and groups: a town that was among the first in the United States to racially desegregate its schools. We were the first "nonprofessional" family to be accepted into a two-county chapter of Jack and Jill, Inc., a national African-American social and educational organization. I remember being told that although I was in sixth grade honors English, I couldn't have written a book report about *The Rise and Fall of the Third Reich:* it was too long and too "complicated" for my family to have purchased and for me to have understood. I had my first official "boyfriend"—the son of the superintendent of schools—a quiet, shy White boy. I remember hearing on the radio, seeing on television, and being confused about the "racial tensions" in our country.

My memories of the 1960s and 1970s are vivid: being in the first coeducational class at a small eastern college; being one of nine Black women in a student body of two thousand; being the only woman and sole Black in most of my classes. Making a new friend during Freshman Weekend and crying when she called to say her mother wouldn't let her room with a Black. Being the head resident adviser, a member of the McKelvy Honors Society, and a Black person who is a woman and who believed in standing beside (or even behind) her (Black) man because "he needs me to counter his castration by society." Spending time in the "Black House" on campus and marching for civil rights; getting sexually threatened by drunken White boys after a fraternity party; being physically threatened by a group of five Black women for being "not Black enuf." Hearing something about a (White) women's movement and getting married to a Black man.

Memories of the 1970s and 1980s are just as strong: Being among a few Afro-American women at graduate school in New York City and the only one in my program in psychoanalytic psychotherapy. Getting divorced and dating old friends. Hearing the word *bisexual* and being surprised that not everyone identified that way. Being a woman who is an Afro-American and who can stand aside from (or even in front of) her man because "we women have been denied too long and really can stand by ourselves." Being the only Afro-American at my first professional social work job and then the only Afro-American who was part of the management team of a small but growing community mental health center.

Later, being one of two African-American women in my doctoral class; working with a faculty of all White men in a program that visibly embraced and continues to support the development of the many sides of me. Being the only social work faculty member with a background and secondary appointment in the business school; being the only African-American woman tenure-track professor. Struggling to uncover myself as teacher-learner-researcher. Doing diversity training and not liking the way we ask the "hidden minorities" to self-identify publicly but not knowing a better way.

Noteworthy in the 1990s: humbly yet proudly getting the award as Teacher of the Year; being asked to serve on the board of a national organization for teachers of organizational behavior and kindred management disciplines; being accepted into the W. K. Kellogg National Fellowship Program; getting tenured, promoted, and then appointed to be the first "African-American woman" dean of my school; receiving the George Washington Kidd Class of 1836 Award for distinguished professional achievement from my undergraduate college (and yes, being the first woman and first African-American to receive that award). Realizing that in most professional schools, the junior faculty and faculty of color are assigned to teach the diversity courses; working with my colleagues to have our diversity course content reviewed; having the course cotaught by *all* faculty. Being self- and other-acknowledged as an ever-evolving teacher-learner-researcher who uses the praxis of reflection and practice as the basis for my class formats and research designs. The story continues. . . .

Lifetime Preparation
Myrtle Bell

The most salient factor in my life is my Blackness. It makes me adhere to the speed limit, keep my car inspected and tags current, and do everything in my power to avoid being stopped by a policeman. It makes me most different from the dominant group in U.S. society. It is what people see first when they look at me. My perspective is always that of a Black person first, a female second.

I learned to do the diversity work I do as a consequence of being Black and female, living my life in a country that places more value on people of race and sex other than mine. My life has provided powerful experiences from which I learn. From the past, I remember saying the Pledge of Allegiance every day in elementary school and wondering why "liberty and justice for all" did not include Blacks. Somehow, even at a young age, my heart and mind were attuned to inequity.

Because of my Blackness and femaleness, I feel as if I have been preparing for the diversity teaching-learning journey my whole life. My perspective toward the work is shaped by growing up in the sixties and seventies in the Deep South. African-Americans were Negroes then, later Blacks; to those unaware or resistant to change, we were "coloreds." Race and rights had a strong influence on my development. Older family members participated in sit-ins at lunch counters in my hometown and were arrested. The slogan "Say it loud! I'm Black and I'm proud!" brings memories and a smile but also twinges of pain.

One of my earliest memories of being negatively seen as different because of race happened when I was six years old. It was the mid sixties. My uncle was arrested in my hometown of Baton Rouge, Louisiana, ostensibly for speeding. He had a convertible Triumph—a TR6. The police jailed him, called him "boy," beat him, and flushed his head in the jail commode. When he finally got his one phone call, he called his boss at the Justice Department in Washington, D.C. My uncle was a civil rights lawyer, employed by the U.S. government. One call from the Justice Department got him released. During the trial, it was demonstrated that my uncle could not have been driving at the "clocked" speed. The officers were shown up for what they were.

That experience left an indelible mark on me. Because of the color of my uncle's skin, policemen who are charged with helping people chose to hurt him instead. I shudder to think of what happens to Black men with fewer resources. Twenty years later, when a White policeman came to my house after an attempted break-in and comforted me, I was reminded that policemen, like all people, can be good or bad. Still, the power of my uncle's experience in the mid sixties remains with me. From it, I had learned to recognize and expect differences in behavior and attitudes within and across groups.

Collaborative Learning
Bonnie Betters-Reed and Lynda Moore

Our journey as two White girls coming together to research, teach, and consult on differences and similarities among women has been anything but linear and sequential. We share similarities of race, yet come from different cultural backgrounds. We came to consciousness of majority and minority group differences in different ways and at different times in our lives. Though our experiences around race, gender, class, ethnicity, and nationality are different, we share similar values and learnings about our culturally bounded identities. The interweaving of our personal awareness and professional experiences individually and collectively has resulted in a collaborative learning process between two White girls who have chosen a lifelong focus on the issue of diversity among women.

Lynda's Story

I grew up in the South in a heavily patriarchal society but within a strong family and a matriarchal culture. I was surrounded by strong female role models, notably my mother and grandmother. My grandmother was the first White female registered stockbroker in the United States. She told wonderful stories. Using her feminine intuition, charm, and keen sense of markets, she was highly success-ful in a traditional man's world. I received strong messages from my grandmother and mother that girls could be whatever they chose, so long as they did not forsake conventional marriages and loyalty to the traditional roles of wife and mother.

Being a southerner, racial consciousness was always part of my life. Racial dynamics, however, were singularly Black and White. I recall no awareness of ethnic differences, although religious differ-ence was pronounced among my White Anglo-Saxon Protestant friends in the Southern Baptist and Episcopal churches. Although I came from a White upper-middle-class background, I was sensitized to my racial and economic privileges and the importance of help-ing those without. My Southern Baptist socialization, combined with my father's values, made a powerful impact on me to "do the right thing." My father reminded us that we were lucky to have material possessions. He made sure we understood the values of hard work and of service to those "less fortunate."

This same message was reinforced by Jesse Jackson when he re-turned to his hometown of Greenville, South Carolina, to speak during our high school race riots. It was then that I joined a student race relations coordinating committee and made a strong public political statement about the responsibility of Whites to discuss racial conflicts. This was a turning point for me. I no longer wanted to participate as a leader in my sorority because of its racial and class elitism. My choice of friends shifted to activists and those whose liberal ideals I shared.

My feminism was further developed through attendance at a women's college, where I was first exposed to women's studies and engaged in the women's movement. Feminists and activists on campus were my friends. We discussed sexism and racism and formed life bonds. In retrospect, it is clear that these conversations were mostly among White women. I studied abroad, expanding my understanding of cultural identity to include national and ethnic components as I traveled throughout Europe. The required cross-cultural adaptation was painful but liberating. My "culture shock" as an ethnocentric teenager in Paris was intense. I became aware of the "ugly American" and questioned my own national identity.

At Antioch, where I pursued a master's degree, I consulted with women's centers integrating feminist theory with organizational change and management. I also did individual career counseling for women and girls. I still remember the day I found *The Managerial Woman* (Hennig and Jardim, 1977). I knew after reading several paragraphs that the topic was what I really wanted to study. I entered a doctoral program at the politically active University of Massachusetts at Amherst.

My doctoral dissertation focused on women managers. Simmons College, home of the authors of *The Managerial Woman*, offered me a job: I was thrilled. The opportunity to return to a women's college, as well as design and teach a course on managerial women, was too good to be true! My explicit contract with Simmons was to critique the management curriculum for its relevancy for women. Later, I co-led two national organizations, the Women in Management Division of the Academy of Management and the newly created Institute for Women and Organizations. My commitment to individual, organizational, and systemwide change has remained constant throughout my career.

Bonnie's Story

I grew up in a small, White, middle-class community in upstate New York. It had a patriarchal culture, all the more reinforced by the overriding presence of our family businesses in town and my three older brothers. In our town, the Italians lived on one side of the tracks. We, the Anglo-Saxon Protestants, lived on the "better" side. We had single-family dwellings, fathers with white-collar jobs, and mothers with washers and dryers—community symbols of socioeconomic success. As a child, I remember wonderful days at my friends' houses "across the tracks" as their grandmas cooked in the basement kitchen, yelling at us in Italian and lovingly attending to our needs. I could not understand why my mother thought our TV dinners were so great when my friends had fresh-plucked chicken and homemade pies. I was naively unaware of ethnic, economic, and class prejudice at play.

I was raised with the Protestant work ethic. I hear my grandparents' and parents' voices in my own as I pass on their stories of the Great Depression, "walking to school," and "fighting over the last can of tomato soup." We never talked about our changing economic status when I was growing up, but rumors circulated around town about our increasing wealth. I tried not to act different.

Just as we never talked about our growing wealth, we never talked about my father's French Canadian heritage. I knew my family came from the Adirondack Mountain region but have only a dim recollection of my great-grandfather's speaking French.

The student revolution of the late sixties and my student teaching experiences prompted me to enter a helping profession. With master's degree in hand, I took a job two thousand miles from home at the University of Texas, Austin. I found myself totally immersed in a different culture. The campus was newly integrated, and among many responsibilities, I directed an orientation program for Chicano and Black students. I worked with a largely White staff and struggled to help different marginalized groups: older returning students, veterans, minority students, gays and lesbians, the disabled. The real challenge, however, was getting in touch with my own racial and cultural identities through extensive training and development. The most profound learning experiences came from students who took great delight in giving me frequent and intense culture shocks.

I thought I was so liberal after my involvement in campus protests surrounding the U.S. invasion of Vietnam and Cambodia. I thought having a lesbian friend during my master's program, who helped me embrace my feminine identity by confronting homophobia, made me a feminist. I thought accompanying my parents on international business trips moved me beyond ethnocentrism. But my Black, Chicano, and White students at UT-Austin taught me otherwise: I heard them challenging this Gringa to "walk her talk."

Ten years later, as I completed my doctoral work at Boston College, I left student development work but not my commitment to marginalized groups. It now seems strange that until this point, I was keenly aware of diversity issues regarding race and ethnicity but not gender. I acted like a strong female leader and was assumed to be a feminist. I had certainly experienced gender discrimination in my own family and our businesses, but I cannot say I had a feminist identity or even a female one back then. I saw myself doing well *in spite of* my gender.

Three events created a new path for me: my long-term relationship with Lynda Moore, teaching and mentoring women students, and being the mother of a special-needs child. Nothing has helped me internalize the lessons of diversity more than the simultaneous joy and pain of a child who is different from the mainstream. It has changed the way I teach diversity: I now live a dimension of marginalization that helps me identify with my students and them with me. They know that even though I am a privileged White woman, I "get it" because I feel it.

Our Identity as Women and Our Work

We have worked together for more than nine years as close friends, colleagues, and professors of management at Simmons College, an undergraduate women's school in Boston. We are both married with two children. Although both marriages have been characterized by nontraditional career norms (for example, both husbands followed us in career moves), we took on the major responsibilities of motherhood.

We both had children in our mid-thirties, after careers were established, and eagerly anticipated the joys of motherhood. We both continued to work full time through the birth of two children, keeping up high levels of research, service, and teaching while juggling the increasing complexity and amount of household and child care responsibility. We never seriously questioned whether we should slow down, although we discussed it intellectually and joked about it.

We vividly recall working late into the evening, sacrificing personal time to get professional work done. With few resources and no infrastructure for course preparation or research at teaching-centered Simmons, we used managerial positions or personal resources to buy student assistant time, secretarial support, and so on. The effort required to teach, research, write, and consult has been intense, the sacrifices many. In the words of Anne Wilson Schaef, we had bought the myth of the white male system (Schaef, 1981). We were dedicated mothers, employees, professionals, managers, wives, sisters, and daughters. We shared a strong sense of loyalty and commitment to our organizations, professions, and families. Combined with our strong personal work ethics, we were constantly exhausted.

As we grew closer personally, we began to share our increasing frustration with the quality of our lives. Points of redefinition for our personal identities were pivotal and occurred differently for each of us. While pregnant with her second child, Lynda was denied tenure and suffered a back injury that made her housebound for two months. She eventually won the tenure fight but reexamined her institutional loyalty and professional commitments. Later, recognizing the inordinate toll of leadership roles in two national organizations, two young children, a frequently traveling husband, teaching, and other diversity-related consulting jobs was another critical step in "letting go." Professional activities and family responsibilities left Lynda continuously exhausted, in poor health, and questioning the value of "doing it all."

For Bonnie, the acceptance of major leadership and managerial responsibilities also coincided with the arrival of her two children and her husband's promotion and increased demands at the office. As Management Department chairperson in a time of retrenchment, she inherited a complex job. Family businesses only added additional fragmentation and pressure. With a second child and the increasing complexity of her first child's special needs, Bonnie realized that the stresses were too great. After a year's sabbatical, she resigned as chair and returned to a faculty role with more flexibility. Letting go of the family businesses was another milestone.

During all this, we increasingly recognized that our career and lifestyle choices were advantaged and that the dilemmas of work and family balance were those of many other White upper-middle-class feminists. The White superwoman's trap, though poignant for us, did not reflect the daily dilemmas of other women with different economic and personal backgrounds. We found ourselves increasingly sensitized to these differences as we struggled with our own dilemmas. Our evolving definitions of our lives and our work reflect these learnings.

A Reconstruction of Self
David Boje

My sense of self is intertwined with my wild ride as a youth. At the core of my being is unfinished business. I do consulting and training workshops, not because of some profound interest in diversity, but to reconnect with the story of my internal self in the past. I want a new story for myself. The time is right for me to work on my teenage self on welfare, reconciling it with my adult self as a professor. I am crossing my own bridge. I cross back in time to live again with my mother on welfare. This time it will be different. This time I am a man, not a boy. I must do this. I must connect to my past. I must heal the wounds once and for all. I realize that this journey is a reconstruction of myself. Before I can change the system, I must change what is deep within my own soul.

The social stigma of poverty and welfare was overpowering to me, as it is for any youth. For over seven years, each morning, I have repeated self-talk to myself: phrases like "I am healthy." "I am happy." "I am terrific." "I am a loving and joyful spirit." I have to say these phrases a hundred times a day to counteract the negative tapes that play so easily. If I can create new self-talk, then I can create a new life script for myself. It is a tough battle.

On welfare, I got into trouble as a teenager and several times lost my personal freedom. Of course, not everyone on welfare does this, but I surrendered to rage and rebellion. My consciousness was shaped by my resistance to the welfare state. Once after being arrested for underage drinking and rowdy behavior, I went to court to face the judge. My mother showed up, even though I had moved out a year earlier, and said, "Your Honor, this is an uncontrollable child." I spent my nineteenth birthday, Christmas, and New Year's in jail. In fact, I stayed in jail for thirty-four days. My life was following society's script for me.

A Process of Relearning
Linda Calvert

I learned about the irrationality of racial hate long before I thought about doing diversity work. I grew up in the Deep South during the civil rights era. I heard about "separate but equal," but I saw unequal. My father was one of the first government workers to be sent to race-related sensitivity training in the 1950s. Thereafter, he was often at the center of controversy, asking tough questions and turning up the heat to create high-pitched "debates."

In college, the civil rights movement reached a peak when James Meredith entered Ole Miss (the University of Mississippi). Many of the students at Mississippi State (where I was) said, "Send him here, so we can get on with classes." One of the great stories of that year was how the Mississippi State basketball team evaded the governor's court injunction designed to keep them from facing "integrated" teams in the NCAA playoffs. Nearly everyone on campus listened to the news as the "B string" was sent to the local airport where the injunction was served, while the "A string" drove to Memphis and flew to the playoffs.

After college, it was marriage, major moves, and a career. A few years into the work world and graduate school, I ran into difficulties. I knew I could do anything I set my mind to, so I tried different strategies to deal with my various "problems" and continued to look for ways to "do it right." Somehow, what I did just did not seem to work that way.

I was asked to teach a workshop for women in management. I resisted; it wasn't my area of interest or expertise. I finally agreed. It later developed into a "Women in Organizations" course. Slowly, I began to understand my own organizational experiences and "problems" in light of what I was teaching.

During this period, I also participated in group dynamics work and other forms of self-development. I began to give voice to my reality and experienced a growing rift with people who assured me that what I saw and felt was not true. I grew. I began to understand better the dynamics between men and women in organizations. I saw that the playing field is not level for women and men and that neither fully grasp the extent of the obstacles.

I read the emerging "women in management" and feminist literatures and found feminist perspectives on language, socialization, power and politics, and competition especially enlightening. I began designing classes and exercises to help women build their own self-awareness and provide opportunities for them to examine feelings, values, and choices.

Race and ethnicity issues were usually part of workshops I took during this period, particularly at National Training Labs (NTL). In my own teaching, however, "diversity" beyond gender was largely missing. Friends and colleagues became my teachers over time and helped me expand my definition of diversity, relearning things I had known much earlier. There were professional conferences with diversity workshops and many late-night discussions with other women. I began to build the bridges I needed. I integrated my experiences growing up with what I learned about being a woman in this society. I integrated my personal development work with my growing awareness of how women friends and colleagues—of all races and ethnicities—experienced the world. I learned to do the diversity work that I do from living, working, reading, opening my eyes, and having patient and honest friends.

Inner Strength in the Way
Cliff Cheng

One of the most personal parts of my diversity work relates to masculinity and femininity. I am not trying to become hegemonically masculine or re-create patriarchal Confucian masculinity. Masculinity and femininity are both parts of my humanness. In and of themselves, they are not desired end states.

In university and consulting contexts, we only work on crude humanness, the lower self. It is the goal of many religions, however, to attain enlightenment. This is often defined as spiritual androgyny—a balanced and graceful flow of complementary aspects of life force (chi), equality of ying and yang. It is only when I have achieved such spiritual androgyny that I can love all the parts of me, especially my Chineseness, and love all that is in my world. Attaining balance, however, marginalizes me in the crude modern world.

I have never been a patriarch—never had the chance. I am not regarded as "man" in hegemonically masculine, dominant terms. Among "oppressed peoples," I am often even more marginalized by their acts to preserve rigid gender roles. Other Chinese men think of me as someone "rocking the boat": I should assimilate, become a "banana"—yellow outside, white inside. Most women, even many so-called liberated ones, do not know how to relate to a man who is nonhegemonically masculine and nongay in friendship, let alone in romance and marriage. Research indicates that Asian-American women assimilate, outmarry to Euro-American men, and get plastic surgery to erase their racial markings (to make their eyes and noses more like those of Euro-American women) at a rate higher than their male counterparts.

In the end, I stand alone and find inner strength in the Way.

Personal Challenges, Professional Interests
Dina Comnenou

One of the most transforming events in my life took place late in my teen years. In a quick and seemingly fated turn of events, I was given the opportunity to study in the United States.

I was brought up in a traditional and affluent family in Greece, where women were powerful but had no professional lives. I never saw myself working outside my home. My job was to become educated, marry, be useful to my community, and honor the values and beliefs of my family and culture.

In high school, for example, I developed an interest in architecture. When I mentioned it to my parents, they explained that architecture was a man's field. I remember their words: "Even if you become the greatest architect through training and talent, you will never be accepted. You will always work for men and fight them to exist in the field. We don't want you to be unhappy. If you want to work, learn shorthand, typing, and business skills to help your uncle in our business." I tried to follow their advice but lasted only a few months before choosing to study liberal arts at Pierce College, a bilingual American college program in Greece.

I was always intrigued by the U.S. culture and was thrilled when, at the beginning of my second semester at Pierce, my academic adviser announced that the college had obtained scholarships for all ten students in my class to take junior year abroad in the United States. A few months later, I was a student in America, despite my family's objections to a woman leaving home at such a young age.

The initial excitement of coming to the United States changed to painful awareness of the struggles to merge my experiences as a young Greek woman with the reality of a small, academically rig-orous women's college in Maryland. American culture was filled with choices and wonder, yet it felt harsh and unforgiving. Com-petition took the place of study groups I had known back home. The pace here was fast and unfriendly. My coping skills seemed in-adequate; my self-image as a bright, resourceful, and competent per-son crumbled under the weight of the culture I so ardently tried to learn. I took long, tear-filled walks around the beautiful suburban campus. I was terrified of failing my dream.

My journey evolved from there. For me, friendships and inter-action helped fill conceptual and informational gaps between the two cultures. Learning about similarities and differences with oth-ers gave meaning and context to my new experiences. As growth is never linear, there were steps backward as I engaged in integrating the old knowledge, the old me, with the new. I was learning to be a person in two cultural contexts. The experience captivated me.

The most powerful dimension of my transformation occurred only a few months after beginning my studies. I was employed as a psychiatric aide in an all-Black hospital during the beginning stages of desegregation. Although I had been aware of the existence of racism and discrimination, nothing could have prepared me for the horrifying and devastating oppression I witnessed. That experience decidedly framed the focus and direction of my work.

What began, then, as an unexpected journey filled with per-sonal learning became my career and life's work: my professional interests have grown out of personal challenges. I have pursued questions and issues from my own struggles to negotiate an effec-tive cross-cultural existence. I have confirmed, through my own life, that cross-cultural transition is positive when resources are available to encourage learning and support is there to manage the pain and intensity. Learning to exist in two cultures moved me intellectually from a single to a multiple reality paradigm in my own life and work. It provided me with data and the impetus to modify and expand my values and beliefs. It offered me opportunities to teach others about the process, integrating my own learning further.

I currently negotiate four cultures on a daily basis: my Greek culture, the southern African-American culture of my husband's family, the British culture of my closest relatives, and mainstream American culture in the northeastern United States. My life and work are integrated and rewarding, yet demanding and intensely challenging.

Insights from Personal Experiences
Peter Couch

I am a White, middle-class male in my early sixties. I've always considered myself a tolerant person, respectful of others, liberal in social views. My parents were social workers. When I was growing up in the 1930s and '40s, we were concerned about problems of the poor and unemployed and sympathetic to the "Negro cause." Although I didn't fully recognize it at the time, my parents held feminist views. As I got older, though ready to espouse values of tolerance and equality, the reality was that my White middle-class world included few contacts with poor people, Blacks, or women in professional roles. My college psychology courses, academic training in industrial relations, and 1960s sensitivity training experiences affected my intellectual understanding of the issues. They did not, however, generate the insights and appreciations that come from personal experience.

I have always found myself in a world of opportunities—opportunities that I thought were available to anyone energetic and capable. I wasn't totally naive. I knew that those outside the White male category didn't always have access to all opportunities, but that was easy to ignore. I could function well in my own world; I didn't know many people who were struggling just to get a fair chance.

A catalyst for change occurred a few years ago when my academic department hired its first female department chair. As I worked with her and learned more about her background and experiences, I began to see the contrast between the problems faced by men and by women in professional careers. Getting to know someone who has had distinctly different life experiences, and in this case, learning about some of the barriers my friend had to overcome, gave me a new awareness of gender issues. When the opportunity arose to sit in on her graduate seminar on women in management, I found myself the only male in a group of sixteen.

Several things happened during that seminar. I read Anne Wilson Schaef's *Women's Reality* (1981). I found her ideas exciting even when they challenged me to look at myself in a less than flattering light. Schaef raised questions that I should have considered long before in my relationships with my wife and daughters. Her views on the "White male system" and her discussion of male and female differences were disconcerting enough to cause serious reflecting. I read additional feminist literature and realized how oblivious I had been of the struggles women and minorities face. It is easy for some of us to go through life not seeing the problems of others, especially when "their" problems don't create problems for us. For White males who live in a world where opportunities seem natural, being oblivious and unperceptive about the problems of others is especially easy.

The Valuing of All Differences
Marcy Crary

Marcy Crary, Earl Avery, and Duncan Spelman teach workplace diversity courses together at Bentley College. Their entries offer insights on teaching issues from the perspective of a diverse teaching team. At times throughout the book, these educators speak as a team; at other times, they speak as individuals. Here, Marcy tells the origin of the group's work together, highlighting a description of the course they teach, its evolution, instructor roles, and more.

Our course, "Managing Diversity in the Workplace," is an elective for both undergraduate and master's students. We first taught the undergraduate course in fall 1990; we offered the first graduate section a year later. We usually do a graduate section every fall and an undergraduate section each spring. (New professorial hirings and adjunct appointments in fall 1995 allow us to offer both the undergrad and grad sections during the same semester when desired.) We usually have forty-five to fifty students enrolled in each course.

The initial development team in 1990 for the course included Earl Avery (assistant to the president of Bentley College and Bentley's Equal Educational Opportunity officer), Duncan Spelman, Barbara Walker (then international manager of diversity at Digital Equipment Corporation), and me. Digital offered initial financial support for course development. To get Bentley's approval to team-teach with four faculty members, we merged two sections into a larger one. We continue to staff this course with a diverse teaching team of four using at least one adjunct faculty member. Our present teaching team is Carole Thomas, Earl Avery, Duncan Spelman, and me.

Our diversity course is largely an outgrowth of the course "Women and Men as Organizational Colleagues," which I had offered at Bentley since the early 1980s. In 1989, I became uncomfortable dealing only with gender. I had met Barbara Walker through the planning of a preconference workshop on cultural diversity and career development for a national professional association and had sought her help in a research project on intimacy in the workplace. In the spring of 1990, she and Bill Hanson (then vice president of manufacturing at Digital) came to the gender class to discuss their work at Digital on diversity. Hearing about their "valuing differences" work made opening up the course to include differences beyond gender obvious. At the same time, Duncan Spelman was heavily involved in staffing diversity workshops in corporations for Elsie Y. Cross Associates. He brought a keen interest in broadening the course to include racial issues.

My relationship with Barbara and the power of the work she and others had been doing at Digital challenged me to rethink our offering to students. The gender focus of the initial course opened students to new ways of seeing and understanding themselves and their worlds. It now seemed odd that we did not consider race and other differences as well. It became clear that our majority group identities had blinded us to other powerful differences.

The move from teaching gender to teaching diversity is significant for me in my own personal and professional development, as well as in the development of the course. Barbara Walker was adamant that we focus our teaching on valuing all differences—not reifying any one as the most important. Doing that means inspecting majority and minority dynamics in any given situation to see how differences are played out.

Early Learning About Differences
Joan Gallos

I grew up in an intense, tight-knit ethnic community in New Jersey. I knew from an early age that I was Slovak and that ethnicity was an important part of who we were. Stories from the Old Country were repeated regularly at family gatherings. Relatives peppered conversations with Slovak terms and phrases. Family celebrations and holiday traditions were firm and clear. Notes, for example, on the intricacies of Christmas Eve supper were written and passed down to me and my cousins, complete with recipes and instructions for table setting, sequencing of courses, history to share, and the symbolic meaning of the foods and ceremonies involved.

Growing up with attention to ethnicity taught me at an early age to recognize differences. By grammar school, I could determine an individual's ethnic origin by hearing his or her last name. I was particularly skilled in distinguishing the national origin of Eastern European surnames—whether someone was Hungarian, Czech, Slovak, Russian, Polish, and so on. I learned this implicitly from listening to the adults around me. For example, throughout their lives, when meeting or hearing about people, my parents' first question was always their ethnic origin. It wasn't a pejorative question. It was honest interest in knowing something basic and important, from their perspective, about who the people were.

I learned about the importance of differences as a child within a context of acknowledging similarities. For years, I was sure we were related to just about everyone I came into contact with on a daily basis. We were "European cousins" to many. The term was used for people to whom we were distantly related or whose families had come from the same small villages as my grandparents in what was then Czechoslovakia. The term was also applied, however, to all the relatives of someone whom, for example, one of my grandparents might have met on arrival at Ellis Island; someone who had helped a grandparent when they first came to America; or a kindred Eastern European immigrant neighbor or friend. There were differences that made us unique but similarities that bonded us together as family.

An Anomaly to Everyone but Momma
Colleen Jones

The fact that I am a college professor is an anomaly to almost everyone except my mother. I was raised in a solidly working-class home. My father was a construction laborer. My mother had various jobs, most often bartender in neighborhood clubs ("corner joints," we called them) when she wasn't a domestic worker. Momma and Daddy made my destiny clear at an early age. I knew I would be a "working woman"—the only issue was what job. After the usual series of career inquiries by relatives and family associates, I learned that the harder the occupation was to pronounce, the more impressed folks were (and the quicker they would leave me alone). So at various points in my youth, I would respond jazz organist (age eight—after mastering the accordion), newspaper reporter (age twelve—after being captivated by a twelve-part series on Africa and a reporter who invited me to come meet with him when I called and asked to see his trip photos), nuclear physicist (age fifteen— after surviving basic physics and declaring myself a genius), and "I'll decide after freshman year" (age seventeen—after college postponed the urgency to answer).

Despite my early-life career lottery, Momma always knew I'd end up in a classroom. I resisted the notion. The only teachers I knew were my own teachers, and I knew I didn't have the temperament to deal with a class filled with students like me. My teachers were great people, seriously dedicated and caring, solid Negro women and men, good role models. Even so, I couldn't see myself being like them. College teaching was something that never entered my mind: I didn't know enough to think about it! I met my first Black Ph.D. when I went to college.

As a Negro child growing up in Kansas City, the "heart of America," in the 1950s and '60s, it was common for the job a person took out of high school to be the job from which one retired. Opportunities were widening for my generation; we truly believed that America was becoming a place where we could "be what our talents willed." Nonetheless, I had no clue as to what that meant for me. Becoming a teacher or a nurse (which is what smart Negro girls did) were possibilities, but my parents had no money for college. My dreams seemed limited by financial reality.

At my all-Black high school, I noticed graduating upperclassmen heading off to college and learned that people without money could go. I was an able student and began to see myself in college too. Once college appeared on the horizon, I wasn't going to settle for being a teacher. I wanted to go where no other Negro child had gone before (at least not in my family). I would study business and then own one. Momma was happy that I wanted to follow her advice and study something to get me a "sit-down job"—to a barmaid and domestic, any job where you sat down most of the time was the measure of success. In conversations with her friends, however, she would regularly add, "But if this business thing doesn't work, she can always teach!"

With Momma monitoring my destiny, I made certain to avoid education courses. The thought of becoming certified to teach would send me back to the books to study statistics or finance. I would *not* become a teacher!

Despite my denial, something happened to me in college. I found myself becoming a "spontaneous educator"—teaching those who had little experience with racial differences through my interactions and daily living. After thirteen years of attending all-Black urban schools and living in a neighborhood with few White families, I purposely chose a large, nonurban state university of 18,000 with only about 150 Black students to test myself and my academic abilities. Opportunities there abounded for me to teach spontaneously about differences. By choosing the college environment that I did, I unintentionally initiated the genesis of my evolution as a professor.

The Dominant Culture as Foil
Gordon Meyer

I recently discovered a life theme about me and difference and gained new insights into how that theme has evolved over my adult life. The theme has endured through decades, but my expression and feelings about it have changed.

I have, from high school days, used the dominant culture as a foil to which I actively assert my difference in visible ways. When I was in high school, for example, I grew a beard before facial hair on young men became common. It was my personal challenge of the dominant adult culture.

As an undergraduate, my need to assert my difference was met through the oppositional student culture and activities of the day. I was involved in student protests of U.S. involvement in Vietnam at a state institution where the dominant student culture was still relatively conservative.

Between college and my master's-level study, I spent three years as a drug and alcohol abuse prevention specialist in rural Pennsylvania. At that time, drug and alcohol education were heavily influenced by law enforcement and medical perspectives emphasizing harsh communication of factual knowledge about the hazards of use. Our approach focused on growing psychologically healthy people. We were counter to, even critical of, the prevailing approach: we emphasized self-esteem, skills, positive child-rearing practices, and humanistic education. Once again, my professional identity and pride were rooted in seeing myself as different.

When I left chemical abuse education to work on my master's degree, the culture of Brigham Young University provided a wonderful foil to which I could assert my difference. There are far too many stories about that to include them all here, but permit one illustration from my first semester at Brigham Young. Like all new graduate students in my program, I was expected to do a project to learn about organizational behavior. I chose power and politics in organizations with a heavy emphasis on labor-management issues, asserting that management and human resource departments act as "servants of power." It didn't take long to see that most faculty and students in the program were relatively conservative, not ideologically committed to the American labor movement, and not inclined to talk in terms of social class.

When I moved from graduate school to a job at General Motors, my identity continued to be informed by asserting my difference. I drove an old Volkswagen or Datsun. I was livid at a memorandum asking us not to comment or bring credit to J. Patrick Wright's book *On a Clear Day You Can See General Motors* (1979) and its depiction of the corporation's culture. I let that be known. I resisted norms that white-collar employees distinguish themselves from "hourly employees" by dressing in business suits. I even got feedback that to achieve my potential as a GM employee required upgrading my dress. They noticed that difference.

I left General Motors after two years, having found the GM culture oppressive. I was eager to study in a setting more to my liking. I chose the Ph.D. program at the New York State School of Industrial and Labor Relations at Cornell. I delighted in the radical critiques by the likes of Richard Edwards (1979) and Harry Braverman (1974). I also found a new foil—students and faculty devotedly pro-worker and pro-union. Suddenly, I was defining myself as moderate (that is, different in a different way). I found myself representing management perspectives. What irony in light of my earlier identities!

In organizational studies, most academic opportunities are in schools of management. Therein lies my present sense of difference: I see myself as a teacher and a sociologist more than a management educator. I often feel more in common with humanities faculty than colleagues in schools of business. While on the faculty at Bucknell University, for example, I cotaught a prerequisite for management or accounting majors. MG 101 is an experiential, realistic preview of management studies. It was not unusual for students to rethink a management major after taking the course. I took pride in providing a provocative and unsettling experience that pushed students to question their choice of major. Some of my management colleagues, however, critiqued the course and my advising: I was "turning away" management majors. I stood proud and in opposition to the excessive careerism and instrumentality of much undergraduate education.

A Necessary Part of Life
Jean Ramsey

I have experienced difference all my life:

- Growing up as a tomboy on a farm with a brother; being like him in every way I could; later moving to town and finding out that girls were supposed to act differently and that brothers prefer to play with boys when they're available

- Living with my mother, two sisters, and brother after my father died; being the poorest family on the "right side of tracks"; realizing that not having a store-bought dress until I was eight (a function of being self-sufficient farmers) wasn't the same as getting hand-me-down dresses from girls whose families were better off financially

- Being the first woman from the "right side of the tracks" to get a divorce in the history of my small town

- Experiencing overt discrimination in the early 1960s as a divorced single parent with three children—apartments were suddenly unavailable, automobile insurance rates increased, and so on; being told divorced women were likely to be "mentally unstable"

- Moving with my three children to New Mexico, where I learned that not everyone is White—Anglos are the minority group in New Mexico (in numbers but not in power); being surprised and dismayed to find that bilingual education meant insisting that Hispanic children speak English but not having Spanish classes available for Anglo children until junior high or later

- Being a "nontraditional" student when I started college ten years after high school

- Discovering that there had never been a student "like me" (divorced, sole support of three children, poor) in the history of the University of Michigan M.B.A. program; being told I was almost denied admission to the Ph.D. program because faculty were certain I would not succeed due to these demographic factors alone

- Being the first woman to receive a Ph.D. in organizational behavior (and the third or fourth to receive a Ph.D. in any discipline) from the University of Michigan Graduate School of Business Administration

- Being the first woman to receive tenure in the Department of Management at Western Michigan University

- Being the first woman department chair at Illinois State University

- Renouncing "upward mobility" and the "pioneer" role I had played for so long; looking instead for happiness and peace

- Being tenured and teaching at Texas Southern University, a historically Black university

These experiences and others have shaped who I am and what I do. My present goal is to understand more about who I am, including my Whiteness, and to integrate that more fully into what I do as a teacher and writer.

Diversity for me is a necessary part of life—one from which I become more whole as a human being. I don't teach "special" diversity courses anymore. Diversity is simply a natural part of everything I teach. I can't imagine it any other way.

Deeply Rooted in Family and Values
Duncan Spelman

My roots in diversity teaching are in my family and in my era. I inherited from my parents the belief that society can be and should be improved. This belief was reinforced by coming of age in the 1960s. I was shaped by forces that taught that social action is feasible and important.

These commitments simmered throughout my preprofessional life, with occasional episodes of activity, including a college semester-in-the-city program and summer work for Ralph Nader. They influenced my choice of organizational behavior as a field of specialization.

As I began my professional life, serendipity intervened. I was assigned to share an office with a woman colleague. We had wonderful conversations about gender in the workplace, leading to collaborative writing, conference presentations, and the like. Gender led to race and a recognition of other forms of diversity. At each successive step in my learning, the rewards were enormous—stimulating colleagues and challenges, richness and variety, and vistas not previously seen. Not surprisingly, the rewards have made me want to dive deeper. As I have done so, my life has become fuller and richer.

Passions for Learning and Self-Discovery
Barbara Walker

We began pioneering the work that is now called diversity at Digital Equipment Corporation in the late seventies. A group of us on the staff of a senior vice president for manufacturing took risks to learn how to talk about the significance of race differences among us. The manufacturing organization had major concerns about the federal government's affirmative action requirements. It was also concerned about issues of productivity in its "minority" plants. I was hired to lead the work.

We began the work with ourselves. In small groups, we told and listened to one another's stories about the impact of racial and gender differences in our lives. As the process unfolded, I learned more than I imagined I could about other people and their differences. But the person I learned about the most was me.

I was a civil rights lawyer when I joined Digital in 1979. I had become a lawyer in the early sixties the hard way: going to law school full time while working full time. My first child was born the year I started; my second child, the year I finished. I was married and played (or tried to play) the role of the traditional wife, at least serving my family home-cooked meals every day.

As a Black woman civil rights activist coming from Washington, D.C., I began work with my Digital colleagues convinced that I had a lot to teach. As the learning-to-value-differences process unfolded, I realized how much I was learning and changing. I was diversity's best student.

Little by little, I discovered that no matter who we are, you and I are on the same journey. We are all looking for truths, asking critical questions, seeking meaningful answers. We're in this together and our differences are a valuable resource as we work together. Suddenly it became so obvious: everyone has something important to contribute; we all hold a piece of the puzzle.

Somewhere along the way, I recognized that learning and self-discovery are my personal passions—especially learning in the service of personal growth and change. At the heart of diversity is a question about one's ability to build interdependent working relationships with people one regards as different. This question raises fundamental personal growth issues about one's capacity for love, intimacy, forgiveness, risk taking, power sharing, and so on. As we did our initial work together at Digital, we broadened our view of our own self-interests and, in the process, developed meaningful authentic relationships with one another.

Preparation

We asked contributors to talk about how they learned to do the diversity teaching they do. We have already seen that a basic form of preparation—a metapreparation of sorts—was forging a strong identity, knowing oneself and one's roots, understanding and feeling the depth of social forces that affect all lives, and embracing a respect for human dignity and equity. We knew from our own experiences, though, that there was more to the picture. Many management educators feel confirmed in their identity, embrace equity and fairness, and know themselves and the world around them. They are not, however, confident or skilled in knowing how to support and challenge students to explore differences and similarities in the human experience, nor do they feel easily able to develop those skills. We wanted insights into what makes the difference. What kind of preparation builds skilled teachers and trainers of diversity?

Good diversity educators are not made overnight. Mentors, role models, and colleagues encourage the development and fine-tuning of skills and understanding. Experimentation and opportunity offer testing grounds for new pedagogies and possibilities. Books and resources feed mind and soul at necessary junctures. Perhaps owing to the evolving nature of the diversity teaching field or of the professionals involved in this project, few contributors found the necessary preparation in formal coursework or academic training, although for some, training in human dynamics provided a natural "bridge" to the work. Most gained the most powerful lessons from other individuals and their own life experiences. All suggest *the importance of persistence and practice in identifying and listening to others on similar diversity teaching and learning journeys.*

Rolling Up My Sleeves and Cleaning Out My Ears
David Boje

I learned diversity work from two mentors. The first was Dr. C. Z. Wilson, former vice chancellor of student affairs at UCLA. He invited me to do diversity training for student groups on the UCLA campus and teamed me with a Black educator, Leroy Wells, from Georgetown. Our racial differences made us a great team. C. Z. then sent me out into the community to *really* learn something about diversity. Over a three-year period, I went to East L.A., Watts, the Oakwood section of Venice, and countless other areas to study the emergence of Black and Latino leadership. C. Z. was a great coach. He knew I needed a lot of training to be any good at diversity.

On one occasion, I interviewed Ted Watkins of the Watts Labor Action Coalition. Ted Watkins is the guy who, when the City of Los Angeles expanded the airport and proposed tearing down scores of houses, put those houses on wheels and moved them across town into Watts. As we toured the community, he'd say: "You see that house there? That green house is where we moved when the city lifted the covenant on where Blacks could live. Did you know that till after World War II, there were housing covenants saying no Blacks, Hispanics, or Asians can be sold these houses? You see this street here? What do you notice? How does it feel to you?" I remember thinking and looking as hard as I could. Finally, I said, "Bleak to me. There are lots of buildings, but no trees." As we drove around, I learned that after the Watts riots in the 1960s, Ted and his organization helped the residents replant all the burned-out trees. I never realized what a difference trees make. When we drove down streets with trees, I felt calmer, more at ease. It was the trees. "I could introduce you to guys who remember planting those trees with their fathers. Do you think anything or anyone is going to touch those trees now?"

Ted Watkins works with the gangs. He hires youth that no one else will to work on moving and building homes. He has his own urban renewal plan. Instead of putting people in public housing, you help families get low-cost mortgages at a few hundred dollars a month. Then you make the senior citizens security guards, set up a fence, and install a gate with one way in and one way out. As Ted says: "People don't want to live in a place without good security." Then you have the gangs, the youth, work under the supervision of union foremen who really train them in carpentry, cement work, and the trades. The kids can learn discipline and have pride in what they do.

Ted Watkins took me to his development, then to one the city built. The city did not provide security or involve youth or senior citizens. It did not require the people to live in the houses they bought. When we drove through Ted's development, there were freshly planted flowers, kids playing on the lawns—it all felt safe and ideal. When we drove into city developments, the lawns were a mess—no shrubs, no kids. Instead there were broken doors and ripped screens. Most of all, every other house had "for sale" on it. I learned something fundamental about diversity from these outings: it takes different types of people to make a successful community. I also learned a deeper lesson: you have to listen and respect the knowledge of people like Ted Watkins who come out of these communities.

The second mentor for me is Nora King. For five years, I went one—sometimes five—times a week to work with her at the Resident Management Corporation of Nickerson Gardens. She is like a mother to me. I do not know anyone better at teaching diversity. She leads with vision, passion, and intelligence. She is also about the most forceful and dynamic person I ever met. I have seen her take on the mayor, a congresswoman, and heads of several city departments to get things for her community. She invited me to work with her and her board on strategies for developing small businesses for residents, getting jobs for residents in the city's housing bureaucracy, bringing student tutors from my university to work with the kids, and getting the Peace Corps to come to Watts public housing. Day in and day out, she schooled me in diversity. "David, you got to take these things before the people. You cannot sit here and make these programs by yourself. Get the residents involved with you. This way we will acquire some of your knowledge. This way the residents won't be dependent on outsiders." Before I knew it, I was standing in a gymnasium with residents in chairs and bleachers; I was explaining programs I was trying to develop, asking if residents wanted things like that, taking names of volunteers to work beside me. Everything I did had to involve the people. We did get Loyola Marymount students to tutor kids aged six to fourteen in math and English. The Peace Corps did come and, with the aid of a grant from the Knight Foundation, three Peace Corps Fellows are working there now doing small business and leadership training. Not only that, they are being schooled by Nora King, just the way I was. Scores of people have gotten jobs.

All I had to do to learn was put aside my professional training as a professor, roll up my sleeves, clean out my ears, and start working with people who were different from me. The strangest thing happened. After a few lunches, dinners, projects, and a lot of laughs, we became good friends and differences between us did not seem so great anymore.

Finding My Way with Help from Others
Marcy Crary

I taught a "Women and Men in Organizations" course for many years at Bentley. I learned about how to work gender issues in the classroom. As more men came to the course, however, I felt uneasy not having a male instructor involved as well. I asked a male colleague, Duncan Spelman, to work with me on numerous occasions. I met Barbara Walker (then international manager of valuing differences at Digital) in 1987, in the context of planning a workshop at a professional meeting. The next year, I asked her to our gender class, along with her boss at the time, Bill Hanson, to talk about the valuing differences work at Digital. After that one session, I realized that addressing gender in our course was not enough. We had to look at other issues like race as well. A new era of learning began for me. It felt different from teaching about my own group identity issues.

In spring 1990, we asked Barbara Walker to join us in designing and team-teaching a diversity course at Bentley. She helped set up a core group (Walker and Hanson, 1992) for seven of us on the Bentley campus to have a place for us to do our own work on diversity. She had a very clear, well-developed philosophy and pedagogy for "valuing differences" learning. It was direct, personal, and experiential. She loved to engage people wherever they entered the conversation and always seemed to have a sense of the next developmental step in those interactions. I was in awe of her comfort in navigating through what seemed to me high-anxiety-provoking terrain. In the process of working with her individually and on our team, I learned better how to "be with others" in our work to value difference. I learned to observe and reflect on my own process of judging others. Barbara was an artist at making the undiscussable discussable and keeping people safe in the process.

In the initial design of our diversity course, Duncan also brought a philosophy and strategies for diversity education from his work with Elsie Y. Cross Associates. We adapted a number of the experiential exercises from their workshops for the classroom, and in the process I learned about ways to examine my own race and gender issues and to work these issues in groups.

Learning from Multiple Sources
Darlyne Bailey

I have learned to do the diversity teaching I do through interweaving talks with friends and colleagues, reflecting on my personal experiences, and reading the life experiences of others. This has led me to consult with several organizations, further fine-tune the process, and then train with a nationally known diversity training agency. And I'm still learning.

Opening My Eyes, Ears, and Heart
Peter Couch

My diversity work is not based on any formal academic program. Much of the academic training I've had over the years in industrial relations, organization behavior, psychology, and the other social sciences, however, is relevant. Conferences and meetings I've attended have been helpful. Most important, however, have been contacts with colleagues, especially one person who played a mentoring role in helping me learn about feminism; reading; and cautious experimentation in classes. I know I've picked up insights simply by observing and listening to students. When eyes are open and ears tuned in, the world is a daily source of data and opportunities to reflect.

Beginning in My Childhood
Gordon Meyer

I learned some of the values associated with diversity work in my childhood home. Both parents were thoughtful about seeing their children exposed to a wide range of people. Other experiences, like a National Training Laboratory (NTL) summer program on laboratory learning and my graduate student years at Brigham Young University, have been important sources of feedback on how my actions are seen by others. Important relationships with close friends and colleagues have also enabled me to see myself as one who can be effective in doing "diversity work." My confidence and self-image as a diversity educator have been significantly shaped by women and minority colleagues who have made a point of telling me when I have been helpful in seeing that different views are valued, that people who are different are not dismissed, and that my support is important to them.

I can also identify one major source of intellectual ideas that undergirds my commitment to diversity. A favorite undergraduate professor was the social philosopher David Norton. His concept of *daimon* from the ancient Greeks has stayed with me for more than twenty years.

The Greeks called one's ideal possibility *daimon*, which had several important characteristics. First, one's daimon is inborn, an individual's "true self." If one follows the great Greek imperative "Know thyself," one seeks the daimon. Second, the daimon exists within people as possibility: self-knowledge is not a *fait accompli* but a direction for growth. Everyone is responsible to actualize this internal ideal possibility progressively. We grow and stretch toward what the Greeks called our destiny. Each person's daimon is unique—a form of perfection differing from every other (Norton and Kille, 1971).

My commitment to learning about and doing diversity work is a manifestation of my personal journey to actualize my daimon. But more important, it is the source of my commitment to a humanistic society in which others are equally enabled to actualize their unique potentialities.

Learning from a Rich and Textured Life
Colleen Jones

The richness and texture of my life taught me about diversity. Growing up in a structurally (and, for a time, legally) segregated environment provided an experience of difference that no formal education could rival. My parents' values, life experiences, perspectives, and love also contributed to my ego strength and self-concept—essential prerequisites for diversity teaching. They taught me that doing what was right, just, and fair when White people treat me badly would make me the better person. They taught me that racism and discrimination were not my problems unless I accepted them. I understood early in life that my choices, standards, achievements, and behavior could influence those unfamiliar with "colored people": interactions with me would make them think, and, ideally, behave, differently.

Learning over Time
Duncan Spelman

My learning began explicitly in graduate school when I was exposed to "process" issues. I believe sensitivity to interpersonal and human dynamics in interactions across differences are essential to good diversity teaching.

The next important venue for my development was (and is) working with Elsie Y. Cross Associates, a consulting firm specializing in diversity. I have learned content and concepts, intervention strategies and approaches; most important, I have learned about myself.

As a member of a teaching team at Bentley, I continue learning in a different setting with a different audience. It is true that the more you work with diversity issues, the better you get. There is no substitute for time and variety of situations encountered. The ability to see and understand issues, one's comfort in knowing how to respond effectively, and acceptance of social discomfort all increase.

Living as Ongoing Learning
Myrtle Bell

Life continues to provide experiences from which I learn to do the diversity work I do and which I can share in my teaching. For example, I recently referred a heating repair company to my mother, a middle-aged Black woman. The middle-aged White repairman went to her large, well-decorated custom home, looked at the heating unit, and wrote down his recommendations for repair. He told my mother to give "them" the diagnostic note and to have "them" call if there were questions. Puzzled, my mother asked who "they" were. The repairman replied, "The owners. Aren't you the maid?" When my mother told him she was not the maid but the owner, the repairman was so flustered and embarrassed he could not function. My mother called to tell me what had happened. The Black female in me was enraged that a company I had recommended made such a stereotypical assumption. I made a mental note to call the salesman with whom I had originally dealt. My mother calmed my anger and said that she could handle it, having ridden on the back of the bus in her lifetime.

I related this story to my undergraduate personnel and human resource management students. I noticed heads nodding and eyes widening. One White female said she could not believe that that had happened in 1995. Several White male students astutely suggested that the company may have supported racist attitudes.

The story had clear implications for students in the course. We focused on training employees not to make discriminatory assumptions and the potential costs in lost business. We talked about this man's need for diversity training. We discussed how organizations make similar assumptions about jobs appropriate for people of color and females and the financial implications for those groups. Our class ended with suggestions for curbing these kinds of occurrences in the organizations in which we work. We all left that class having learned more about diversity.

Being Diversity
Cliff Cheng

I am on the diversity teaching and learning journey, for I have nothing to lose. My racial uniform cannot be taken off. The color of my skin, the shape of my eyes, my coarse black hair, the way I express myself, how I see things, and most important, the ways in which I am not perceived by others as being a "real man" in White male, capitalist, patriarchal, heterosexist, Christian terms mark my non-belonging. As an "other," a scapegoat for the projections of White racism and White wanna-bes, I learned fast and hard about diversity work. This is learning by the emotional and physical terror of racism and masculinity discrimination—an often unacknowledged form of sexism directed against marginalized men.

Several critical incidents influenced me to go on and prepared me for the diversity teaching and learning journey: immigrating to the United States, discovering I was an "other," being called "nigger"—I am Chinese, but the people in my all-White elementary school had never seen someone of color before—getting beaten for being a "chink" in my multicultural junior high school, trying to conform to White male norms but discovering the best I could ever hope for was acceptance as a token.

There will always be triggering events that make me feel the anger and fear I have around diversity issues. If I repress my feelings—as many intellectuals do and as I used to do—I pay the price in my ability to relate intimately with people, in my creativity, and in my health. I then have nothing genuine to offer others. I need to feel the whole range of human emotions, from rage and racism to love and rapture, in order to welcome diversity. Only then will the pain weaken. It will never go away: it is in my memory and my unconscious connection with humanity.

Diversity teaching starts with *being* diversity, even for White males. To *be* diversity, one must confess being both victim and perpetrator. As far as I can tell, we are all connected by the mass unconscious of racism, sexism, classism, homophobia, religious intolerance, colonialism, and much more. These isms reside in archetypal forms and interconnect humanity through individual unconsciousness.

The Experience of Being "Othered"

*E*ducators bring different knowledge and perspectives to the diversity teaching and learning journey. Some understanding of diversity issues is academic and intellectual. An equally important source of knowledge, however, comes from personal experiences as members of socially defined groups. Age, ethnicity, sex, physical ability, race, sexual orientation, socioeconomic class, and other demographic factors are neutral descriptors until society sorts, clusters, labels, and evaluates people "of a certain kind." These social grouping processes powerfully affect individual lives. They influence opportunities, behaviors, status, values, beliefs, and worldviews. They shape life and interactions in the workplace in strong and often nondiscussable ways. They result in some individuals being "othered"—being seen as different in some way from the "mainstream."

As the stories of the contributors in this section poignantly remind us, being "othered" is painful. So is the self-reflection necessary for transforming pain into learning. None of us are members of a single identity group; we are all simultaneously members of multiple groups. We move in and out of dominant and nondominant group status. At different times, one or more group memberships may be more central to our self-concept or more noticed by those around us. Our willingness to grapple with the implications of all our group memberships, however, is essential for the personal authenticity demanded in the diversity teaching process.

Many contributors to this volume talk about "being" a form of diversity and living it on a daily basis. Their physical characteristics are

constant reminders of their "otherness" in society. Some have less obvi-
ous group identities and face conscious decisions about when, what, and
how much information about themselves to reveal. For those whose group
memberships are seen as more "mainstream," powerful learning often
comes from the experience of being "othered" on some dimension of dif-
ference. Our various group experiences combine to shape how we think
about and teach diversity.

Tellin' White Folks About Black Folks
Colleen Jones

There were five Black women out of five hundred students in my
freshman year dormitory. I had two White roommates. One was
from a suburb of Chicago. On our first day together, she informed
me that she had once dated a "Negro boy." My other roommate was
raised on a farm in rural northwestern Iowa. After four weeks of living together, she told me she had never seen a "live" Black person.
I dismissed the "date" reference but was shocked by the revelation
of my rural roomie. What would it have been like never to have
seen, talked to, or interacted with a White person? *Never.* For the
first time, I realized that the world I knew probably had no anchor
for a large number of White people. My roommate was an example
of many other Euro-Americans in the late 1960s. Like her, they
knew very little about Black people from direct observation, interaction, or experience. It seemed necessary, then, for Euro-Americans
to learn through school and other intentional interventions what
people of color learn from just being alive.

On Sunday nights, for example, I would go down the hall to the
showers to wash my hair. It became an important dorm ritual: I'd
return to my room to find four (and sometimes up to nine) girls
there to watch me "press and curl" my hair—that is, before my
Afro emerged second semester and the girls just wanted to touch
my hair, asking, "How do you get it to stand up like that?" These
"beauty shop" conversations became my floormates' orientation to

Black life in America. I, who never saw myself becoming a teacher, took on a role of spontaneous educator. Departing from conversations about hair, we would discuss food, what life was like growing up, role models, political ideology, aspirations, sex, athletics, and, of course, music. In about three hours, my hair would be done, the peanut butter crackers and vienna sausages would be gone, and my White floormates had insights into Black life. We were learning about each other's cultures and lives in a very personal and meaningful way.

When I talked with other Black students on campus, I learned that we all had experiences "holding court" and "tellin' White folks about Black folks." As we recounted these "culture classes," we often smiled at the naïveté of our White peers' perspectives and questions. Occasionally, those sessions were painful or the friendly conversational tone became contentious. As we "brothers and sisters" talked about those, one of us would exclaim, "Why don't they understand? How could they not know? I'm sick of being these folks' Black Cliff Notes!" I remember feeling tired of teaching about "the Black experience" and wondering, "Why can't these White folks learn about me like I learned about them?"

Wearing a Racial Uniform
Cliff Cheng

In students' teaching evaluations and comments to department chairs, I am often criticized as disorganized, not getting to the point, not controlling the class, and so on. For years, I thought it was because I was a part-time, temporary instructor hired at the last minute: textbooks often didn't arrive until midterm, and secretaries did not type my syllabus or copy my class materials as they did for full-timers. Clearly, my part-time status and service issues were significant. After colleagues watched me teach, however, and told me that by their departments' standards, I was doing a "good job," I began to suspect that part of the issue for students might be a lack of awareness of or even intolerance for my culture and style. I have tested this hypothesis by administering evaluations of my own at various points during the term. When I force myself to use a Western, linear style and slick sound bites, my evaluations go up. When I use a style more natural to me—more intuitive, flowing, open-ended— my evaluations go down.

Well-meaning colleagues have told me that I can't afford, financially or careerwise, to take chances, develop my "classroom as a high-involvement organization" simulation, or do highly experiential diversity teaching. Even if I wanted to, however, I cannot play it safe. My race, culture, and nondominant masculinity cannot be turned off. Students will always make an issue of the "foreign" way I think and express myself. The first reaction of many when they see me walk into class on the first day is, "Does he speak English?" For this lifetime, I wear a racial uniform that permanently marks my nonbelongingness in the so-called First World. The people who judge me—students, administrators, colleagues—know by looking at my "slanty" eyes, coarse black hair, and smaller physical size that I'm not one of them.

Being Dismissed as the "Other"
Gordon Meyer

In fall 1979, I enrolled at Brigham Young University (BYU) as a student in the Masters of Organizational Behavior program. A primary reason for choosing BYU was the opportunity to live in another culture. I knew little about the Church of Jesus Christ of Latter-Day Saints (LDS, or Mormons) but had little doubt, once the application process began, that the Mormon culture was different from mine in fundamental ways. The BYU admission process, for example, included an interview with the local LDS bishop and a signed pledge that, if admitted, I would abstain from alcoholic and caffeinated beverages, abide by conservative dress and grooming standards, and assist all of my colleagues in fulfilling their responsibilities under the Mormon code of honor.

At the time, however, I knew two things that made the risk of being different at BYU tolerable. First, there were faculty in the organizational behavior program interested in enrolling non-Mormons. Second, I knew that White males were highly esteemed in the Mormon church and BYU. Since there are no obvious physical characteristics to identify one as Mormon, I assumed that I would be able to "pass" as one of the dominant group when I chose. That was true. If I acknowledged being addressed as "Brother Meyer," I could pass as "one of them." The temptation to pass was real: I'd feel no vulnerability in being different. Disclosing my difference generally resulted in attempts to "aid in my conversion" or dismiss me as irrelevant.

The most powerful experience at BYU of being different occurred in classes where instructors routinely drew on examples from Mormon church organizations to illustrate organizational processes and structures. The most painful incident of that kind occurred when one senior faculty launched into his umpteenth such example for the semester, hesitated, and turned to the one other non-Mormon and me. He said something to the effect that he knew we didn't share this background but begged our tolerance and then proceeded to use the example as if we weren't there or didn't need to understand the concept discussed. I assume that the teacher thought this an act of sensitivity. I felt pain being singled out and dismissed as unimportant. I imagine women and people of color feel similar pain when "we" note their difference and then define it as unimportant for "our" purposes. I felt what it was like to be told that I wasn't important enough to be included as anything more than an "other." I'm not sure whether being dismissed is better or worse than being expected to represent the "other." Neither is fair to someone who is different. My behavior in the classroom as a teacher continues to be influenced by my understanding of what it means to be dismissed as different.

Hearing "We Know You're Not like That"
David Boje

I feel uncomfortable when I'm treated as if I'm not there. I notice, for example, during conversations with people of color about the prejudices of White people—"White people are like that, you know how they are"—someone will inevitably turn to me and say: "Dave, we don't mean you. We know you're not like that." I've overheard White people talking about "those Blacks are like this and that" too. In both cases, I feel estranged. I dislike situations where someone is defined as the stereotypical "other."

Sometimes I get carried away with this. I was negotiating the renewal of an employment contract with city department heads on behalf of the community. I started saying, "We think that the contract should include this clause about no rent increases for trainees." "Where do you get off using 'we'? How do we know what you say reflects the people of Nickerson?" "I use 'we' because we work together on these things. I have been before the people and solicited their input, and if you don't buy that, call Nora King. She will tell you herself."

Why was I getting so worked up? Why do I still find myself saying "we" in my conversations with insiders and outsiders to the Nickerson community? It is more than just working together. I share the same dysfunctional family history as some of the people at Nickerson. We are the people who do not like to sit down at meals with the family because sit-down meals trigger memories of bad times around Mom's table. None of us had strong father figures at critical times growing up. "We" have these experiences in common.

Unearthing Taken-for-Granted Assumptions
Marcy Crary

One of the major lessons for me in diversity work is how easily we are blinded by the assumptions and judgments we make about our own and others' group identities. An example of this is a story about a panel I was on for our alumni chapter. The session topic was "Diversity at Work: Managing Within Our Own Identities." On the panel with me were a Black woman and a lesbian White woman. In preparing for the session, I went through the following thought process: "OK, we're going to discuss gender, race, and sexual orientation. I guess Sara will do race, Andrea will do sexual orientation, and I'll do gender. Now what do I want to say about gender?"

Midway through this thinking, I stopped, shocked at what I was doing. I made the Black woman responsible for race and the lesbian for sexual orientation, as if I had neither of those group identities. The power of the moment was seeing how I was forgetting to name and see my own Whiteness as part of "race" and my own heterosexuality as part of "sexual orientation." In addition, I was ignoring Sara and Andrea's gender identities. I automatically "assigned" the nondominant group members responsibility to represent and address the issues of difference. This was a powerful moment. My own ability to see my blindness came from working with others on these issues, in the classroom with my colleagues and our students.

Part II

Understanding the
Diversity Teaching Terrain

What Is the Work?

*T*he phrase *"teaching workplace diversity"* has been used to describe many things—from short workshops about race or gender to corporatewide strategic initiatives on valuing all differences, from classes on demographic issues to integrated treatment of diversity throughout university degree programs, from workplace lectures about *"everyone getting along"* to long-term explorations of the connections between diversity and productivity and competitiveness, from psychologically oriented perspectives on individual and interpersonal awareness to more sociologically based studies of systemic and policy issues, and more.

Variety in teaching approaches, foci, and definitions of the work is essential in an area as complex as diversity education. So is clarity about options and possibilities. Managers and organizational decision makers need information about a full range of educational alternatives and prospects in order to make informed choices. Educators explore a range of options for expanding skills and expertise and identify new areas for growth and development. What are the options for diversity education? What is the work?

To answer these questions, contributors were asked to define the diversity teaching work they do. Their responses provide appreciation for the breadth and variety of the field and point to the evolving nature of diversity education. Some contributors, for example, define their teaching as encouraging dialogues among individuals; others create structures that bring people together in new ways or new configurations to explore similarities and differences. Some focus on the individual and advocate deep *self-reflection; others target systems, groups, and organizations. Some use their recently discovered voices to experiment with diversity issues in their teaching and training; others describe complex ongoing efforts. Some teach by initiating active interventions; others respond to serendipitous opportunity. All see effectiveness as dependent on the fit between teacher, learner, and specific institutional context, needs, and constraints.*

Such differences among diversity educators are no surprise. The highly personal nature of the teaching and learning process, ongoing development in understanding workplace diversity issues, pedagogical preferences and experiences, and distinct entry points to the diversity teaching arena all interact and lead to different perspectives on what constitutes "the work." Lack of formal preparation and training for diversity educators, fueled by tendencies to view diversity education as a liberal luxury, only increases the variety. In such an environment, many of the contributors to this volume have pioneered the field.

A Broadly Defined Task
Barbara Walker

In all my years of doing diversity work, I haven't discovered the best way to define it. I define the work so broadly that I get into trouble. Today so many people want short sound bites and unambiguous answers to complex questions. "Tell me what I have to do. Just give me the quick short version. What happens? How will I know when it's done?"

The work of learning to value differences comes in many forms with many dimensions. Trying to define it reminds me of the age-old story about blindfolded people describing an elephant. They feel different parts of its body. The one touching the leg says it's a tree, the person with the trunk thinks that it's a fire hose, and so on. Some people think of diversity work primarily in terms of the victim-oppressor relationship. Others think in multicultural terms—learning about differences in cultures across the world. Of course, for some, it is dealing with inequities in the ways society treats a particular group.

I think diversity work is all this and more—much more. It is the work of learning to value differences among people—all differences, all people. It is more than learning simply to tolerate differences. It is learning to view them as assets and learning how to make the most of them. Diversity work is developmental work—personal and organizational. It is self-actualization sparked by learning about differences, across differences, and from differences. It is a focus on differences in order to learn, grow, and change. The differences among us create a marvelous context for learning. They are agents of change, learning, and relationship building.

A Focus on the Individual
Linda Calvert

My focus in diversity teaching is not learning about multiculturalism, learning about creating diversity, or learning "about" anything in general, although all of that may happen. My version of diversity teaching is to create a structure where people can take a journey within themselves and talk about their experiences with others on a similar quest. The classroom part of this is enhanced by exercises, information, cases, statistics, or whatever best informs the journey. The focus, however, is on the individual—who you are, what you believe, and how that affects the world in which you and I both live. I talk about my journey; you tell about yours. The structure ensures that both of us have opportunities to explore our reality and be heard.

Dialogues Across Differences and More
Earl Avery

Talking about differences is not something that people frequently do, and certainly not with people who are different from them. People typically share differences with folks who are like them and who think along very similar lines. A good diversity course is an opportunity to open up that dialogue. It's a chance to prevent discrimination and harassment when young people get out in the workforce. They might think about things before they do them; that might prevent them from becoming victims, losing their jobs, or costing their corporations or institutions a lot of money.

We talk about acknowledging differences. I think we sometimes fail to realize that through these discussions, we also begin to see commonalities. The issues are complex for all of us: someone can be in one place on one issue and somewhere else on another. That complexity forces me, and I suspect others, to struggle continually with this stuff.

Every day for me is a diversity teaching effort. I don't see separation between what I do in the classroom and what I do every day. Not being cognizant of diversity issues puts me and other people at risk. I'm constantly aware of that. It's the equivalent of asking me, do I think about being Black in America? Yes, I do, every day. In the classroom, curriculum requirements lead to a more formalized kind of teaching. Take away the formalized aspects, and I'd still say I'm doing it every day. I can't walk away from diversity teaching. Even if I stop teaching a specific course, diversity will continue to be alive in my life.

Awareness of Group Identities
Lynda Moore and Bonnie Betters-Reed

We have had to come to grips with our own definition of what a "good" diversity program in an organization requires. To us, managing diversity means all of the following:

- Enabling every member of the workforce to perform to her or his potential by appreciating, developing, and using unique human resources; it doesn't mean controlling or containing diverse people.

- Creating a multicultural organization, a dominant heterogeneous culture; it does not mean helping women and men assimilate into a dominant White male culture.

- Making good use of every worker's potential at every level, especially in middle management and leadership positions; it isn't hiring women and people of color at the entry level, nor is it merely complying with affirmative action legislation.

- Enhancing corporate strategies, improving everyone's quality of work life and the firm's performance in the global workplace.

Most problems in organizations stem from a lack of awareness and understanding of intergroup and intragroup racial, class, and ethnic differences and how they affect business and management. Steps toward solution must be aimed at creating a culture conducive to open communication in order for in-depth learning to occur. Diversity research, training, education, and dialogue must be placed on the agenda for management education in both corporate and university settings. Dialogues about diversity must be seen as a legitimate business issue. A new cultural paradigm is needed for valuing diversity education and recognizing the hegemony of the dominant White male and female value systems.

The focus of diversity education needs to be on helping the mainstream groups change, not on fixing minority groups. This means teaching about majority and minority group identity. Awareness of cultural identity for oneself and others is the first step in building sensitivity to multicultural issues. Personal and organizational transformation begins with personal awareness. Multiple methods or interventions can be used to facilitate such learning (readings, personal journals, structured questions, experiential exercises, ethnographic field research, guest speakers, and so on). The commitment to teaching diversity is a lifelong commitment to learning more about our own cultural identity and that of others. Teaching diversity is difficult, as well as intellectually and emotionally complex. Conflict is inevitable, but it is a natural and important part of the personal journey to understanding and valuing differences.

About Social Systems
Duncan Spelman

The diversity teaching I do provokes people into exploring social systems that sort people into groups and assign privilege or pain based on that sorting. I strive to make the interlocking parts of that social system more visible to dominant group members, who often begin their learning blind or with badly distorted vision. One teaching goal is to facilitate dominant group members' learning about their privilege. Another is to support subordinate group members in coping with a system that is often overwhelming or frustrating—help them do a reality check to assure them they're not crazy, and warn them of the dangers of unconsciously colluding with and reinforcing the present system.

I seek to complement this examination of systems-level aspects with exploration of individuals' personal histories and current attitudes. The goal here is to assist people in understanding themselves in relation to diversity. I strive to help people uncover deeply internalized things they have learned about differences that now feel "natural." I strive to facilitate an examination of current feelings and behaviors in light of formative life experiences.

Finally, my teaching must help learners identify their self-interest in creating change. Addressing diversity-related issues requires courage and persistence. I believe that neither is likely unless people understand why any action is in their interest. The challenge is greater, therefore, for members of dominant groups; subordinate group members have more obvious interests. From my perspective, however, the fundamental instability of systems based on oppression and the profound distortions that result from living with unrecognized privilege are two important reasons for dominant group members to embrace change.

Lifelong Learning About Differences
Marcy Crary

In an overall sense, diversity education is one kind of adult development work. It asks us to take perspective on and question our systems of organizing the world and ourselves, particularly as these systems relate to group identity differences. It is teaching ourselves about the realities of the isms in our society and in our workplaces and about how each of us can be active change agents in addressing inequities. It's about learning how individual, group, and organizational-level phenomena determine and are determined by difference dynamics. It's about waking up to discrepancies in power and opportunities available to dominant and nondominant groups. It's looking at how we participate in maintaining the status quo and feeding organizational systems of prejudice and discrimination.

In our diversity course, we ask students to look at what they and others around them do, think, feel, and espouse with respect to race, gender, ethnicity, physical ability, sexual orientation, and so on. In doing this perspective taking, they are surprised at what they see. They find themselves asking new questions and challenging old assumptions about personal and professional relationships, work dynamics, and organizations. We push students to be alert to differences and to make active, responsible choices in responding to them.

Finally, our course models lifelong learning about differences. We demonstrate the need to create contexts for learning where all feel safe to discuss the undiscussable, explore stereotypes and assumptions about identity differences, and address dominant and nondominant dynamics.

About Interconnections
Darlyne Bailey

In years past, I would have defined my diversity work as simply helping folks recognize and appreciate their own and others' differences. Recently, however, I have begun to honor my ancestors more fully, enabling myself to embrace *all* of who I am and will be. I now realize that all that I do is in honor of the many sides of me—and thee. My present diversity or polycultural work continues to acknowledge differences. It also includes similarities and rests against the reality of interconnections: how my teaching and learning affect others and how others' learning and teaching affect me.

A Recently Discovered Voice
Gordon Meyer

Until recently, I have not thought of myself as doing diversity teaching. I was more inclined to think of myself as one who aspires to but has not done so for a variety of personal and institutional reasons. For the past ten years, I have been a teacher at highly homogenous institutions, a White male who didn't think he had much voice in teaching about diversity, and an instructor largely unwilling to risk student rejection by being assertive about diversity issues. I think of myself as more devoted to learning about diversity teaching. At the same time, I am highly conscious of the issues. My self-identity is of someone who does diversity work with peers by forthrightly pointing out and confronting behavior that I think is inappropriate, rooted in stereotypes, or devaluing of differences.

An Ongoing Process
Dina Comnenou

In graduate school, I wrote a paper outlining the process of cultural transition I had undergone. My academic mentors pointed out that I had articulated a developmental model on the process of integrating two cultures and suggested further research. This work, a balance of personal, affective, and intellectual issues, became the cornerstone of my academic interest in cross-cultural transition and the topic of my dissertation. It also became the foundation for my consulting and academic careers.

Having conceptualized my experiences in the development of this model, I was repeatedly asked to share what I had learned. Soon I was working with schools, colleges, universities, human service agencies, communities, and corporations on intercultural relations and workplace diversity in national and international arenas. Simultaneously, I became interested in teaching about the issues—trying to bring my work and personal life experiences to the classroom. I wanted to learn better how to weave together experience, theory, and research and to develop truly integrated and collaborative learning opportunities for my students.

This is the goal I still pursue in my teaching. It is an ongoing process. New areas and issues emerge as my exploration becomes deeper and more comprehensive with time. As I immerse myself in learning about human diversity and its implications for interaction, teaching, and organizational change, I become more convinced that this is my lifelong journey.

Work That Evolves Over Time
Peter Couch

In the courses I teach, I devote a small portion of time to diversity issues; my objectives are limited. My sense of "diversity work" is evolving, however, gradually broadening to include a wider range of differences. There are two parts to my broadening interests: my own learning and ability to act and my desire to help students learn to understand and act. The ultimate goal in all this is for us to relate "well" to others as individuals. The more immediate task is to gain understanding of categories of individuals according to gender, race, physical abilities, and other dimensions; personal insights for both me and my students; and abilities to resolve problems related to our differences.

Liberatory Education
David Boje

The link between what I do in public housing and what I do in the classroom seems fragile and ephemeral. Most universities shut out public housing residents and others who are different. Students and faculty rarely leave their ivory towers to talk with the poor. The network of discourse that keeps the public housing resident a resident is mirrored by a discourse that keeps the university out of public housing.

The majority of public housing children have never been to a university. The majority of university students and faculty have never been to public housing. Freire (1990) suggests, "No pedagogy which is truly liberating can remain distant from the oppressed by treating them as unfortunates and by presenting for their emulation models from among the oppressors" (p. 39).

Fortunately, Loyola Marymount does encourage faculty and students to reach out to the poor. Colleges and schools of business, long insulated from the poverty class, are beginning community service projects as part of their instruction. The ivory tower is cracking. In fact, we don't even recognize the small ways in which we can hasten that process. Take my conversation with Shirley, a resident leader at Mar Vista, a public housing project in Los Angeles, about including public housing residents in my leadership course at Loyola

Marymount and involving Loyola Marymount M.B.A. students in various training workshops for Mar Vista residents.

DAVID: My leadership class is starting. If anyone wants leader training, let me know.

SHIRLEY: I think I could get Mike and one of the girls to come. Leader training is required before we can get (some kind of support she wants for the gangs).

DAVID: I also want to get a Peace Corps worker started working with Mar Vista. This would be a good time to do a dual management workshop, one just for Mar Vista.

SHIRLEY: There are things I want to talk to you about too. Come by Tuesday afternoon.

DAVID: Will do.

With this exchange, I opened up my classroom to a rich and varied experience. Two public housing residents attended my university class that term. Both are now enrolled in college. They realized that they were bright and wanted to get ahead with an education. M.B.A. students learned from the exchange as well. Many described this as the most important graduate class they had taken. They wondered how they could get more involved in doing something about their community.

Naturally Emergent
Cliff Cheng

I do not teach diversity in the sense of doing or telling something to clients and students. Presenting diversity materials cognitively reinforces the status quo: people intellectualize instead of feel, heal, and act. I do team building and third-party conflict resolution work with groups. We look at the difficulties in respecting and valuing differences.

Through a simulation I developed called "the classroom as a high-involvement organization," I offer people a means to experience the stages of group development. Diversity issues emerge naturalistically, especially in the early stages, when members struggle with defining norms and deciding "who fits in?" and "can I be accepted?" Learners have opportunities in the simulation to look at behaviors and attitudes implicit in their interactions.

Teaching and Learning—Anytime, Anyplace
Myrtle Bell

I define diversity teaching work as any type of teaching that helps any student learn about similarities and differences. Students may be friends, family, or neighbors, as well as those enrolled in a university class or organizational training program.

For formal students, my teaching includes sharing data to help people understand what is actually occurring in organizations. Data, for example, on occupational sex segregation, population demographics, job categories and levels, and management positions help remove naive, equality-based blinders without accusations or personal charges. My diversity teaching work also includes stories about my own life and experiences as a Black woman in corporate America.

In more informal contexts, my teaching work may be something as simple as an admonition to listen to what others say and consider the implications. Many sexist and racist comments are stopped short when people listen to themselves. Other times it's opportunities for deep conversation. My seven-year-old daughter, for example, recently told me that she had learned that her best friend is Jewish. I used our conversation to talk about people who say things like "Blacks don't like Jews and Jews don't like Blacks," explaining to my daughter that her love for her friend and her friend's love for her show the ignorance in such statements. I told her that we must be careful about making blanket statements and including all of one group of people in a certain category. I could almost see her mind working, thinking, and storing.

Rethinking One's Truth
Colleen Jones

The essence of the diversity teaching I do is to provide a context to overcome latent or manifest misperceptions about people, values, cultures, and attitudes. Stated differently, I provide contrast to others' perceptions. I seek to stimulate critical examination of the stress and anxiety that occur when one's expectations are met by an unexpected reality. I offer an invitation to rethink what one assumes as truth.

How Diversity Education Differs
from Other Teaching/Training

Diversity education is different from other teaching and training. Clarity about the differences is essential in order to meet the educational challenges. We asked contributors to explore the differences they see in their own work. Many echoed a common theme: diversity teaching and training require more involvement of self, attention to one's feelings and reactions in the present moment, and the ability to manage deep emotion. Some offered unique takes on the diversity teaching and learning process, such as partnership models and multidisciplinary approaches. Others identified a pedagogical shift over time—the form and substance of their diversity teaching has begun permeating their non-diversity-focused courses and consulting work. Increasing pedagogical comfort with diversity teaching, awareness of a wide range of diversity issues and methods, and commitment to equity can blur distinctions between diversity education and other kinds of teaching work.

Gets You More Personally Involved
Peter Couch

I try to be a "learning facilitator" in all my teaching work. This is especially so in diversity work. In part, I think there is a strong moral component in diversity work, and it seems essential to be open with students about my values. I feel more personally involved, and the issues seem to be more emotional for both me and the students.

Pulls on You Personally
Earl Avery

Teaching a diversity course has a way of pulling on you personally. You can't be detached or just teach theory. If you are a woman, you are certainly affected by gender discussions. Being a person of color, I am touched personally by racial comments in class and in papers. For example, people may make a statement to show how "open" they are. Then they use a word like *colored* or talk about how their parents use the N-word but aren't bigots. This hits me personally. I've got to make a decision about how to respond. Do I take on the issue that something just doesn't fit for me: how can their parents not be bigots if they use terms like *"nigger"*? This calls for a response that your curriculum can't prepare you for. If I taught marketing or accounting, I'm sure the class comments would involve me less personally. They'd more likely be theoretical. Nondiversity courses do not have the ability to cause you pain, joy, concern, or even fear in the same way as diversity courses. They don't require that you extend or expose yourself personally. In diversity teaching, we do expose ourselves.

Brings Teaching Closer to Heart and Mind
Marcy Crary

Diversity teaching feels more personal and "experience-near" to me. I have always tried to make organizational behavior courses experiential and therefore personal. I have never, however, taught so close to the heart and mind—my feelings, values, and perceptions so out on the table and open for inspection—and about issues that have such a profound impact on lives. The issues are "hotter" than those that arise in typical organizational behavior classes. We work to make the undiscussable discussable. That evokes excitement and anxiety. It is an ongoing struggle to create a classroom climate that allows us really to listen to each other, to give each other space to tell our stories, to seek understanding of each other's experiences.

Such personal teaching and learning feels more emotional to me than other teaching. We get students thinking about how they were raised, how they treat and are treated by others, how much discrimination exists in the workplace. Basic assumptions about the world are challenged when hearing about oppression, inequities, and privilege that can implicate us all. We can all have feelings of guilt, shame, embarrassment, sadness. Our work thus requires a balance of support and challenge—keeping people "safe" but confronting realities we may not want to address. We do all this in the context of a typical classroom with students at various levels of awareness and development.

I carry my diversity teaching around with me: it is a lens on my personal and professional life. It has made me more conscious of my own group identity, where and how I live, whom I hang out with, what actions I take or don't take to effect differences in our society. It has motivated a group of us to initiate an institutional diversity change process at Bentley, now in its third year.

I feel strongly about the importance of what we're teaching and a sense of mission and urgency in our work. These are important issues that society needs us desperately to work on.

Demands Being Fully Present
Gordon Meyer

Diversity education requires a clearer sense of self and a greater facility for being fully present in the here-and-now than other teaching. It requires a well-developed and disciplined approach to listening to others on multiple levels. When I am at my best doing this work, it is because I am able to communicate unambiguously that I have heard and appreciate the words, thoughts, or feelings of another who is different from me.

Uses the Self as an Instrument
Barbara Walker

Diversity work is very different from other work I have done in the past. In this work, one uses oneself as an instrument of the work. As teacher or trainer, we become the number one role model for others. We lead by example, fully participating in the difficult discussions, speaking authentically and truthfully, taking risks, admitting mistakes, keeping a sense of humor, and pushing and confronting colleagues in a caring way. When we use ourselves as instruments of the work, we are always threatened by burnout. I personally put a lot of energy into protecting myself from burnout so that I can stay charged, authentic, and passionate.

Makes Other Teaching Seem Bland
Duncan Spelman

Diversity teaching is deeper, more demanding, and more frustrating than other teaching I do. Correspondingly, I feel most alive as a professional when I do this work. The importance, complexity, historical tenacity, and emotionality of the issues can be overwhelming. It also makes other teaching seem bland and almost inconsequential in comparison. I always feel the potential for an extreme incident of some kind when addressing diversity issues; it's more difficult to predict what will happen.

Threatens Necessarily
Cliff Cheng

Most organizational behavior topics can be treated discretely and are nonthreatening. Diversity, if properly taught—that is, taught experientially—is threatening. Teaching diversity as dispassionately as one would teach the Hawthorne studies is ignorant, superficial, or a deliberate avoidance strategy.

Requires More Deliberate Objectivity
Colleen Jones

My diversity teaching differs from other teaching in an interesting way. I am noticeably more measured, tightly organized, and deliberately objective when I teach about diversity. I'm aware that what I am attempting to convey about the issues can be interpreted as a psychological diatribe if I am subjective, blaming, or highly personal. I feel freer to "play" and use avant-garde approaches when teaching subjects like leadership or conflict management. Because I am a Black woman and therefore what most would consider a "diverse" individual, I am careful to balance the theoretical, practical, and personal aspects of "difference." I do not want students or seminar participants to feel that my diversity teaching is somehow too unique or too personal to challenge perceptions or behaviors. Sometimes, I feel my "indigenous expertise" works against me when I strive to teach about workplace diversity.

Involves Partnership
David Boje

Five years ago, we negotiated a contract with the City of Los Angeles allowing public housing residents to obtain jobs in the Housing Authority bureaucracy. We organized training for residents with zero money that avoided the usual dependency trap: getting a community to depend on outside experts and funding.

We created a partnership model. For the first go-round, I worked with the president of the Resident Corporation and several resident volunteers to identify the training required for the new jobs. We interviewed Housing Authority managers and supervisors where resident-trainees would work to identify on-the-job training available. We asked people from the community to facilitate training sessions and assist me and other volunteers in putting on the workshops. This partnering was explicitly designed to transfer knowledge to the residents.

The first workshop trained fifteen people and lasted three days. Seven participants were later selected for the new jobs. After a year on the job, all had excellent performance ratings and were considered among the better employees. The city expanded the program during the second and third years. By the last workshop, ten professors from the business college, seven M.B.A. students, and a dozen undergraduates teamed up with the residents to host seventy trainees from four different housing developments. Residents who assisted during the first workshops now conducted their own sessions on topics such as conflict management and personnel policies. M.B.A. students and undergraduates prepared seminar materials and conducted additional sessions on interviewing and team-building skills. At the end of the training, residents donned caps and gowns and received graduation certificates.

Benefits from a Multidisciplinary Approach
Dina Comnenou

We each make meaning out of the field in unique ways. For me, a multidisciplinary approach has been the most enriching and rewarding route. I find it impossible to present a balanced and substantive picture of the concepts and issues without reaching into literature and knowledge from several disciplines. For me, a multidisciplinary approach reflects the complexity of the work. It also makes my work more personally satisfying and useful to my students and clients.

My diversity teaching therefore reflects a broad spectrum of concepts. For example, I bring management literature into teacher preparation courses. When exploring the development of classroom environments to support multiculturalism, management issues such as power, leadership, and group dynamics are helpful to students. Student teachers seem to have difficulty seeing themselves as professionally powerful. They tell me that helping them identify, articulate, and manage their power is beneficial to them. Examining models of effective group leadership is instrumental in expanding student horizons beyond the alternatives predominant in education. Combining these concepts with cultural diversity, social justice, and multiculturalism provides unique and meaningful learning.

Conversely, teaching management students about the education field enriches their understanding of concepts such as social and cultural learning. It provides viable, practical alternatives for facilitating communication, interaction, collaboration, and the effective utilization of diverse human and cultural resources.

Starts with the Individual and Moves Outward
Linda Calvert

In my teaching, I am always interested in the individual—the individual's style, sense of responsibility, slant on truth, impact on others. When I teach leadership, for example, I think it important for each person to understand her or his own values, preferred styles, and abilities. What are my values as a leader? How do I want to lead? Where do I want to lead? What are my purposes? What makes sense given my style and abilities? With such knowledge, leading comes from a centered self. My "Women in Organizations" class deals intensely with students' personal lives and ties all that into the professional world. More recently, I taught a graduate organizational behavior class with all the traditional management topics embedded in a context of ethnicity, class, gender, sexual orientation, and other forms of difference. Always, I start with the individual then move outward.

Too often people set out to improve the world or simply use it without looking carefully at who they are, the meaning of their choices, or the reality of other people's lives. "Who I am" matters for many reasons, but in this context, it forces me to explore my values and rights in relation to the values and rights of others. I am not naive enough to think I will open the eyes of those who do not want to see. However, I have been amazed at people's eagerness to examine their own values, their surprise in discovering their beliefs, their openness to hearing others' views, and their willingness to grow and change. In a collaborative learning environment where people are evaluated on their willingness to challenge themselves rather than on the basis of where they begin the struggle and what they believe, incredible things are possible. Learning is mutual and growing is less painful when the journey is shared. We all have insights and strengths, as well as failings and blinders.

Influences Other Courses
Lynda Moore

I have taught an undergraduate diversity course for fourteen years and have had the luxury of redefining that course as my personal awareness and professional development around diversity evolved. What began as "Women in Management" has developed into a more complex course dealing with all aspects of diversity. My other courses, too, are heavily influenced by diversity issues. Organizational behavior, for example, focuses on understanding the organizational implications of domestic and international multiculturalism. Two graduate courses, "Communicating Across Cultures" and "Strategic Intercultural Communications," were also designed to provide conceptual understandings, behavioral skills, and awareness in cross-cultural thinking for professional communicators. It has been challenging as well as fun to view the communications, management, organizational behavior, and strategy disciplines from a domestic and international multicultural context.

I have found that all these courses require an enormous amount of research. Good resources on diversity are not readily available. All use customized packages of readings, sometimes supplemented with a text or a popular book. I believe it is important to mix didactic and experiential exercises, educating students simultaneously on cognitive and affective levels. The emotional dynamics in diversity-related courses are always more complex than in any other courses. This requires more interactions with students in and out of the classroom. The courses surface intense emotions about each student's own prejudices and stereotypes, forcing students to examine their cultural identity.

I have also worked to bring my knowledge and skills related to diversity into other consulting assignments. In executive education programs, diversity issues are easily seen when we explore issues like leadership, team development, management practices, oral presentation skills, or our monocultural standards for performance, succession planning, and mentoring.

Presents an Integration Challenge
Bonnie Betters-Reed

Initially, my diversity research and training had little connection with the courses I taught, especially our school's capstone strategic management course. I struggled with how to integrate my interest in diversity with the traditional content of strategy that is more structural than behavioral, more hierarchical and exclusive than all-encompassing. A colleague pointed out that I must challenge my students to read between the lines, think about what is not said, who is not included, and why. That conversation has stayed with me for six years. I have gradually integrated diversity perspectives into the strategy course through my choice of cases, group assignments, and class discussions. The student group projects, like business plans for a multicultural bookstore or customized video book publishing for children of color, are witness to the transformation.

Likewise, integration of diversity perspectives into course content has been a goal in another course, "Communications in Management." This has been easier in a behaviorally based course with opportunities for diverse readings such as *Black Ice* (Cary, 1991). Journal writing, a long-standing tradition in this course, is also an excellent opportunity for students to explore self-awareness and understanding of others.

Touches Every Aspect of My Life
Myrtle Bell

Diversity teaching has deep personal meaning and importance for me, for my future, and for that of my family. For that reason, it is infinitely different and far more important than any other teaching and training I do. Ironically, for the same reasons, it is also inseparable from the other teaching that I do. A diversity perspective colors my every thought, even when I am not consciously aware of it. It touches every aspect of my life.

I therefore intertwine diversity issues into my teaching and training in ways that others, for whom the issues have less personal importance, might not. For example, a discussion about the changing nature of the workforce and its implications for human resource professionals might center around flexible benefits and work schedules but lead to discussion about possible discrimination against employees with family responsibilities. A topic such as the effects of immigration on the workforce might include a discussion of compliance with hiring laws as well as the importance of not assuming that every Hispanic is an illegal alien.

Being Black, female, well educated, and in the formal role of teacher or trainer often adds additional credibility to what I say about workplace diversity. I have firsthand, real-life experiences to share. I am also seen by some as an example of "diversity in action": acknowledging that someone like me can be the teacher or trainer is a powerful learning for some students, regardless of the focus of the class.

Creates Spaces for Multiple Voices
Darlyne Bailey

I am now at the point where the only real difference between my "diversity" sessions and others is in the *primary* content covered. In "diversity" classes, the primary content is a focus on polyculturalism. In all my teaching and training, however, I include content on eradicating the isms, honoring differences, and acknowledging similarities and interconnections. In all classes, I try to facilitate the creation of spaces that make room for multiple voices. In all classes, I model self-discovery with the hope that others will join me. And in all classes, I present myself as a teacher-learner, encouraging all to recognize themselves as such as we cocreate our learning.

Evolution in Definitions of the Work

*D*iversity education is at an exciting crossroad. It is evolving as a new *multidisciplinary field. Advances in our understanding of diversity issues are combining with an upsurge in interest from corporate and academic arenas to create additional opportunities for learning.*

Diversity educators find increasing acceptance of their efforts among the more traditional management disciplines. Twenty years ago, an elective course devoted to women in management issues was seen as progressive. Today, the American Assembly of Collegiate Schools of Business, the major accrediting agency for schools of business and management, makes diversity issues a required part of the curriculum.

Meanwhile, organizations scramble to understand the implications of workplace diversity. Courses, in-house training programs, and a flurry of new books aimed at managers have appeared. Corporate needs pressure schools of business to advance their knowledge and diversity offerings and provide field opportunities for experimentation and program development. Experimentation leads to new knowledge and teaching methods, which in turn foster additional interest in diversity education. We are in the midst of a new wave of attention to the importance of understanding workplace diversity.

In the past decade, we have also learned about the possibilities and limits of diversity education. We recognize that valuing diversity means more than labeling "minorities" as different and attempting to assimilate them into "business as usual." We acknowledge that diversity education encompasses more than explorations of race and gender. We have a growing body of research, curriculum designs, exercises, activities, field notes, and personal learnings to share and examine. Despite the personal and nonlinear nature of the work, patterns are beginning to emerge.

Change, however, involves more than acceptance and the natural evolution of a new discipline and its body of knowledge. As the contributors remind us, diversity teaching also results in personal change: evolution of self, one's approach to the work, and individual commitment to continued learning and exploration. Choosing a personal path for the work is more than a one-shot deal. Options, perspectives, and possibilities multiply with time and experience. While the specifics of the contributors' evolution in the definition of their diversity work varied, their stories contain common seeds: ongoing change and choice.

Shifting Gradually
Peter Couch

I've gone through an incremental process in learning about diversity, gradually expanding my focus to additional concerns. Issues of age, for example, seem likely to receive more of my attention before long. I've enlarged my views about the territory and teaching content. I've shifted from thinking in general terms about problems of the underprivileged, for example, to presenting information and involving students in discussions of issues in class and to gaining increased personal skill and comfort in working individually with students. The scope of my diversity teaching is broader; the focus is deeper.

After working for a few years with the woman who served as chairperson of my department, I sat in on her M.B.A. seminar on women in management. I prepared an informal report as part of the seminar, "Things White Male Professors Ought to Think About When Women Are in Their Classes—and Even When They're Not." I saw this as an opportunity to summarize ideas I was considering. Looking back, those ideas now seem pretty elementary: watching language and word choice, not expecting one woman to speak for all females, never condoning even borderline sexual harassment, not making a big deal when a woman talks about cars or baseball, remaining conscious of gender stereotypes. At the time, it was a giant step toward "diversity literacy." I took action.

Over the next few years, I experimented. I read about subtle gender discrimination in the classroom (Hall and Sandler, 1982) and organized class discussions about the issue. At the time, few students seemed to "catch on." Later, a colleague and I conducted a workshop called "Subtle Gender Bias in the Classroom—Some Thoughts for White Male Professors" at a national teaching conference. Women who attended the session encouraged us to continue our work, pleased that some men were trying to do something.

One class project that enlarged my understanding of the diversity terrain was a "put-down" exercise. I asked students to find real life examples of "put-downs"—behaviors or comments that communicated in any way that another person was inferior. Some examples were frivolous; others were meaningful. When we analyzed three hundred of the examples, we found gender and race references common but were surprised that put-downs dealing with competencies and physical appearance were the most common and often the cruelest.

I began to reevaluate the issues I needed to include in my thinking about diversity. It was easiest to begin with gender issues. Half my students are female. Raising gender issues for discussion did not single out one or two individuals. The scarcity of Blacks in my classes has made me careful about introducing race to avoid putting the one or two African-Americans there on the spot. However, as my own reading and involvement with Blacks on campus has increased, so has my willingness to raise questions of race. Recent contacts with Latino and physically challenged students have further enlarged my views.

One of the difficulties in teaching diversity has to do with maintaining a balanced perspective. On the one hand, balance means avoiding stereotypical thinking, regarding all students as distinct individuals, and reacting to distorted or one-sided views. On the other hand, it requires providing a safe environment for learning while not overprotecting people capable of standing on their own. It means acknowledging that any person can get caught in the trap of narrow, prejudicial thinking.

The evolution in defining my diversity work makes me realize that I need to ask questions at a different level. I need to move beyond asking myself questions like "Why do differences exist?" to more action-oriented questions like "How can one actively value differences? What needs to be done? What can I do?"

Bonding with a New Colleague
Bonnie Betters-Reed

Before coming to Simmons, I designed a "Women in Management" course similar to the one Lynda Moore had developed there. I loved teaching about women and had experimented with "diversifying" the course, in part because the students included men. I felt that the course had much to offer and was just beginning to articulate this when I went to Simmons.

Women in management was Lynda's turf. She knew the field better than I. At the time, she was chair of the Academy of Management's Women in Management Division. I remember sitting in my office thinking how important issues of diversity were for our curriculum and that this might be a topic on which Lynda and I could collaborate. If nothing else, it was clear to me that I could learn from Lynda. I initiated a conversation about the challenges diversity issues posed in my previous teaching experience.

I witnessed Lynda in action. She picked up the telephone and connected with people across the country, building on our ideas as she went. She was a whirlwind of enthusiasm and productivity. What emerged was our first symposium on the dilemmas of teaching diversity, presented at the Organizational Behavior Teaching

Conference. It galvanized our mutual interests, partnership, and working styles. I was the thinker and organizer; Lynda, the connector and spinner. The eventual diversity series in the *Journal of Management Education* that Lynda and I coordinated gave me the opportunity to make a critical transition and to reestablish our partnership on equal ground.

Focusing on the Interface
Dina Comnenou

The interface among cultures, organizations, individuals, and groups is where I now choose to focus most closely. My work life began with attempts to understand differences in cultural background and perspective. I confirmed for myself the significance of exploring these concepts from multiple angles rather than a single paradigm.

I first turned to psychology for a basic understanding of self, self-concept, and identity. These concepts seemed meaningless, however, when explored separately from the social context within which an individual exists. Community social psychology helped me understand that self and culture are not as distinct as I had originally thought. It helped me focus on the relationships among different aspects of human community. In community social psychology, exploring human rights, oppression, and racism is central to understanding group and individual relationships, social justice, and the need for social reconstruction.

Interests in the development of teams, communities, and organizations to support and nurture diverse human resources led me to the field of organization development. I immersed myself in group dynamics, as well as issues of organizational and systems change. What I learned was especially valuable for understanding human interaction and conflict management.

It is clear to me that too often, doing diversity work is interpreted as teaching others without acknowledging the importance of exploring our own needs for learning and change. We stay trapped within our own cultural and disciplinary boundaries, reinforcing our mono-cultural paradigms. Examining our own cultural, organizational, indi-vidual, and group interfaces means understanding "process" issues—how we do things—as a relevant, academic product.

All aspects of our work—the structure of courses and knowledge, the organization of thought and writing—need to be viewed and understood from a variety of cultural perspectives. We cannot talk about conflict as a cross-cultural issue yet suggest monocultural strategies for resolving it. We cannot speak about differences in understanding the world while using monocultural models of orga-nizing and presenting our theories and data. In academia, however, linear ways of thinking, writing, and functioning are still evaluated more positively than nonlinear ones.

Seeking Refuge to Heal
Cliff Cheng

I did not consciously choose my path. Rather the ingeniousness of life, of the Tao, maneuvered me into position to do the healing I needed to do. My path first led me to hide in my head. That was bet-ter than getting beaten up emotionally and physically for being a "chink." Getting a Ph.D. was about seeking refuge in intellectualism and counterattacking the ruling White male Christian capitalist ide-ology—at least symbolically, from my perspective. As long as I remained in my head, it was hard for people to hurt me. I thought that studying the sociological and psychological reasons for my oth-erness would heal me and lead to enlightenment. I could then make a difference in the world as a diversity change agent. It was only much later that I realized that by intellectualizing my feelings instead of experiencing them, I repressed powerful anger and sadness from the discrimination against me.

When repression no longer served my journey, the resourceful-ness of the Tao, life's creative process, sent a plane I was in crash-ing to the ground. My mind could no longer explain away the shame, anger, sadness, and grief of my otherness. Once again I had nothing to lose. I moved faster along the path of Tao, the journey of life.

The despair of being a victim of racism, the shame and sadness of the victim state, and the anger of vengeance are what I am in the process of healing. I move toward a more enlightened energy and vision of a world without isms, a world based on trust, safety, care, intimacy, and love. Diversity teaching gives me a context to do this work.

Acknowledging Polyculturalism
Darlyne Bailey

I have been a trainer and a participant in many "diversity" workshops. I now work with faculty colleagues to revisit and revise the content and design for a required "diversity" course. Though I have coached friends who have written about this subject, I have never put a word on paper about diversity for an academic audience. Several times I have asked myself why, and I answer with phrases like "I don't want to get 'pegged' as writing only about Black stuff," "it's not my area of *scholarly* expertise," and "no one has ever asked me to do that." Now the uncloaked, honest answer is twofold and suddenly quite obvious to me: writing about diversity is writing about my life—joys, struggles, and constant challenges. In addition, I don't like the word *diversity*. Something like *polyculturalism*—a word that spans and connects—works better for me.

Moving Beyond a Missionary Model
David Boje

A major lesson for me from my work in public housing in Los Angeles is rethinking my own imperialist mode of wanting to help others. I invaded the community. I had a missionary model of living with the natives in order to convert them. That's not a good model.

The president of the United States should jog through public housing. He should require the caretakers of public housing—all those high-paid executives and lawyers in Washington, D.C., the armies of white-collar executives in housing authorities across the country—to live there.

A partnership model can replace the missionary model. Nora King, a resident leader at Nickerson Gardens, a public housing project in Los Angeles, taught me to seek community involvement for everything I do. I learned to work differently. I began taking my proposals to community meetings at Nickerson, for example. I started coaching resident volunteers on how they could negotiate with the city. Together, we brainstormed ideas about policies, programs, and strategies. This way when I left, people could do for themselves what we had started together.

Things are not always as straightforward as we wish. When Nora King was put out of her position at Nickerson by U.S. Representative Maxine Waters and her slate of handpicked candidates, neither model seemed to work. Maxine Waters, for example, distributed fliers when Jack Kemp, former head of the U.S. Department of Housing and Urban Development, came to speak at Nickerson. Maxine had hoped to get political control over at least five public housing developments in her district. She bused in residents from another development to protest Kemp and ask for Nora and her board members' withdrawal from the next community election. Signs held at Kemp's speech said that Nora stole money from the community, contracts were being awarded to friends, and money was being wasted. It was strange politics. When Maxine Waters's candidate Pam and her board took over, I had no support to remain in the community.

Nora actually won a seat on the resident management corporation's board, but the residents of Nickerson also voted in Pam and Pam's board members. Nora's board did not run for reelection. After two meetings, Pam consolidated her power and voted Nora off the board. Locks were changed on the resident management corporation's offices, and Maxine Waters's lawyer started sitting in on the board and staff meetings. He and I butted heads. I had to leave or begin again.

I had to think, who am I doing all this for? The residents of Nickerson Gardens. Do I want to be involved with politics? No. My loyalty had to be to the kids who relied on the Loyola Marymount tutoring program, the people attending our job and small business workshops. I decided to stay. Except for one secretary and me, everyone associated with Nora King was fired or resigned.

I did not know what to do. One day, Pam and her board asked if I wanted to come to a Tupperware party. I went. That is how I broke the ice. I ordered a microwave popcorn bowl, joined in the party games, and became a person working with other persons. At community meetings, Nora retained her role as community activist. More than once I stood between Nora and Pam as they shouted at each other. I tried to be a peacemaker. That was new territory for me. I would hold both their hands and speak about the contributions both were making to the community. Nora did accuse me of selling out. I just kept coming back and working with both ladies.

After three years with Pam, no money from Washington, and an all-volunteer effort on the part of my university, there was a new election. Nora King was reelected to resident leadership with a new slate of candidates. I work with Nora again. We managed to keep the tutoring program, the jobs program, and the Peace Corps initiative alive.

Choices of Strategies and Arenas for Change

Educators make choices about where and how to engage in teaching workplace diversity. These choices are influenced by a wide range of issues. Some are unique to the individual instructor or trainer. Others are contextual. A diversity educator's background and personal experiences, comfort in working with particular sets of issues, willingness to take risks, knowledge of relevant teaching strategies and options, and beliefs that certain issues are just too important to ignore interact with the needs of students, clients, and organizational contexts to influence the path and focus of diversity work.

The diversity teaching path is not well charted. There are a wide variety of instructional methods, "classrooms," and issues. The work is complex, emotion-laden, and filled with unanticipated educational surprises. It changes over time. Opportunities to "make a difference" are many. The contributors to this volume remind us that all this makes continual learning and discovery essential to teaching success.

Teaching in Love and Quietness
Myrtle Bell

To a large extent, my personal path to diversity teaching came with the territory of being Black. Maintaining my dignity and self-respect has often meant educating people. Recently, I have become more deliberate, methodical, and purposeful about this. I have learned that it is best to teach in love and quietness rather than anger and rage. I realize that becoming too emotional with audiences harms more than helps. I try, therefore, to distance myself from the personal "rightness or wrongness of valuing diversity" and emphasize the business and economic necessity. I speak more honestly and truthfully about the issues: speaking from the heart has more influence.

My personal goal is to educate as many as I can, one person at a time. In educational, workplace, and personal arenas, I see opportunities to do that. At school, I share personal experiences of racism and discrimination. I have opened the eyes of peers who respect me as competent and hardworking. Rational people with understanding of quantitative methods, they can see that when all potential independent variables are accounted for except race and sex, some of the remaining variance must be attributed to those factors.

At work, I use the same "rational approach" to educate people about diversity. I counter insinuations or comments that I was hired for my Blackness and femaleness with discussions of my performance, education, and training as compared with those who preceded or competed with me for the position. I share data from the U.S. Glass Ceiling Commission (Tomaskovic-Devey, 1994) that at all levels, women and racial minorities have more experience, tenure, and education than males and Whites.

My excitement about the current preoccupation with "managing," "valuing," and "embracing" diversity is tempered by my irritation. Why did we not do these things when it was "right to do" rather than wait until it became fashionable or a demographic necessity? Why must fears over becoming noncompetitive, not attracting the best talent, or facing excessive turnover drive us to think seriously about valuing diversity? Idealism aside, I accept blessings as they come and will do my best to educate before the current furor subsides.

Giving People a Chance to Talk
Barbara Walker

There are many ways to do diversity work. The most exciting, the most effective entry point as I see it, is helping people learn how to talk and listen to one another. Everyone has a story to tell about the impact of differences on their lives and careers. Most people want to tell their story. The heart and soul of this work is giving people the chance to talk.

Even the most private people want to be heard: they may not want to talk, but they do want to be heard. Stories paint pictures. Small group dialogues to tell stories are a safe place to begin the work. Learning is deepened and enhanced when a group of people commit to explore their experiences, feelings, and ideas about differences. These dialogue groups provide two important learning opportunities—a real on-line experience with people we regard as different and a chance to reflect on the meaning of that experience. Dialogue provides a good place to think critically about and sort through stereotypes, assumptions, labels, and habitual emotional responses. A sense of safety develops when people realize that we all have things to teach each other. As people reveal themselves to one another in an iterative process of talking and listening, listening and talking, they deep·n their goodwill toward one another. They learn to be kind, patient, and trusting.

More specifically, when I lead two-day diversity workshops, my approach is to begin with exercises and activities designed to help participants recognize the fact of differences and their intrinsic value. Before working on any specific dimension of difference, it helps to recognize that each difference is a metaphor for another.

Not long ago, I was asked to conduct a valuing differences workshop for a large group of Black and White city leaders. The workshop's managers had assured me that the all-inclusive approach was just what they wanted; they said that the group had already done some basic diversity work. Within hours of starting, however, the group mutinied. They insisted on using their time together to deal with only one issue—racial differences. They made it clear that they had no interest whatsoever in working through any other differences. Since the group was equally split along gender lines, I asked, "Isn't there one person who wants to include gender?" No response. (I later learned that some participants were angry because gender had been excluded.)

I worry that in this country, we'll only learn to value differences one at a time—work on each separately, difference by difference by difference. We view life in terms of its dualism: good (my way) or bad (your way). Instead, I wish we could learn, truly learn, that the fundamental problem is our basic attitude toward difference.

Using Both National and International Lenses
Dina Comnenou

My work as a teacher and a consultant has led me to recognize that doing justice to diversity and cultural pluralism means embracing a multidisciplinary approach. I also need to understand and use literature and resources from both international and national arenas.

My research on cross-cultural transition processes, for example, led me to the work of Clemmont Vontress (1975). Vontress notes that culture shock, a concept widely used at the international level, has enormous significance on a domestic level as well. He speaks of the negative reactions and "culture shock" often experienced by professionals in the United States who work with clients of different cultural, racial, and linguistic backgrounds. The potential for rejection, avoidance, stereotyping, and undermining the different cultural context of clients is predictable and well understood by intercultural practitioners versed in culture shock. There is even support in the literature for these reactions being healthy, necessary, and potentially positive dimensions of cross-cultural transition when appropriate support for learning is available.

Understanding this phenomenon enables me to assist my students in anticipating these kinds of reactions in their work. Despite its usefulness, however, the implications of domestic culture shock are rarely explored by U.S. practitioners and writers in the diversity or multicultural fields. Similarly, I must add, international practitioners do not fully utilize knowledge and experience from professionals who deal with differences, disempowerment, and oppression of U.S. populations viewed as outside the "mainstream."

Finding a Space to *Be*
Cliff Cheng

When I was a student in a graduate seminar, a classmate who was a human resource manager angrily responded to my comment about diversity. "Why do you always have to be different? Can't you just go with the group for once?" I do not set out to be unique, difficult, or radical. I see things differently and notice the lack of community and communion in Westernized societies. My classmate wanted conformity, not inclusion. She wanted me to "get with the program" despite her interests in learning how to help people. (I fear from my experiences with her, however, that manipulating people into conformity "for their own good" is probably more what she intended.) All this is ironic in light of my retrospective realization that I was in that graduate program to heal from getting beaten up for not understanding and fitting in.

Western notions of human development focus on individuality and ego. Taoists are concerned with enlightenment. The focus of Taoist life is the spiritual journey. For Taoists, relationships are ritual. Each individual is a journey person on the other's path—one who assists in learning and growth by being a character in the other's life story. Ideally, Taoists see and honor others as deities.

They must notice and deal with dragons on the path—their own internal dragons in the disowned self, as well as external ones.

The height of many Eastern spiritual practices—Taoist, Buddhist, yogic, and so on—is enlightenment. One cannot become enlightened by rigidly presenting oneself in accordance with rigid gender roles. Spiritual androgyny is an indication of enlightenment. True androgyny is not sexless or lifeless. It accepts and balances the ying (receptive) and yang (active) chi (life force). Meditative practices are a means to deconstruct and disempower such false consciousness as racism, sexism, classism, homophobia, religious intolerance, and colonialism. Patience, not manipulation, dissolves the pain and torment of false consciousness. As this occurs, hypermasculinity and hyperfemininity dissolve through dedicated practice, and passionate living with ying and yang balance.

In Chinese brush painting, the "negative space"—the white surrounding the subject—is most important. To me, space simply to *be* is what diversity teaching is about. This means being the journey person, listener, supporter, and friend of others on the spiritual path. In turn, they will do this for me. Chinese call this *quanxi* (used here in its highest form). *Quanxi* means more than relationships, connections, or reciprocity—these are Eurocentric translations. Kinship patterns among Chinese before capitalism, missionaries, and communism provided what one needed without asking. Care, awareness, and love were nonverbally understood and exchanged at unconscious levels.

Focusing on Diversity Among Women
Bonnie Betters-Reed and Lynda Moore

We spent our first years together exploring the emerging field of "managing diversity" by interviewing pioneers and leaders in the field. Our initial objectives were to provide a cohesive definition of managing diversity and identify teaching and training content and methods for the field. What we found, however, was that general diversity work lacked relevance and challenge for us. We decided to return to our women in management work, this time using diversity as a lens. This offered us the opportunity for original contributions and greater relevancy in our teaching of women and in our own lives.

In 1989, we landed on the topic of diversity among women. We were the first to admit that we did not know what that meant, but it felt right. When invited to participate in a round table discussion on diversity management at the national Academy of Management meeting, we accepted on the condition that we focus on differences among women in management. The resistance we experienced was a sample of reactions to come. The topic was a challenge on all fronts. We had to defend our choice of topic—"Won't this divide women?"—as well as our role as two White women assembling and facilitating a prominent panel of diverse women and men.

To prepare for this round table, we read bell hooks (1984, 1989), Paula Giddings (1984), Johnnetta Cole (1986), Audre Lorde (1984), and Patricia Hill Collins (1990). These feminist authors were all women of color who expressed disdain and dismay over the continued oppression by White male and female organizational hierarchies. It was a painful revelation that the feminist movement, canonized in the women in management field, was White and exclusive. The issue of "White privilege" had powerful implications for our work on diversity among women. Focusing on an equality battle with White male cohorts neglected the experiences of our sisters of color and women outside the managerial ranks.

This was the beginning of a conscious shift from general diversity work in organizations to diversity among women, with a focus on understanding the racial privilege that White women and men have in our society and businesses. This focus on racial, ethnic, economic, and social differences between women of color and White women forced us to "own" our own racial privilege. It was a liberating experience to recognize that as White women we could use our power and positions to discuss White women's responsibility to "do their own work." Our message that Whites have race and ethnicity too has been a difficult lesson for many White women who want only to confront gender differences and their own exclusion from the White male club. That we might be the oppressor and discriminate against other women is something not all White women can hear.

Finding Comfort in Choices of Arenas
Gordon Meyer

As I have thought about myself as one interested in learning and teaching about diversity, I have wondered about the appropriateness of my own relationships with those who are different from me. Why, as a White male, am I far more comfortable exploring these issues with women, and to a lesser extent minorities, than with my White male students and colleagues? I suspect the answer lies in my assumptions about who feels as I do on these issues. I assume that most women and minorities share my attitudes about inclusiveness and valuing difference.

I'm newly aware of my relative comfort in "doing myself" in a way that is sensitive to difference and communicates a willingness to deal with it directly. My greater comfort is in more personal settings than in the classroom. In personal settings, I feel more control and ability to read the social cues.

Discovering Surprises Along the Way
David Boje

I got a phone call from a former M.B.A. student. "Come to Nickerson Gardens. We want you to work with residents who are trying to do something about their children's education and to get themselves empowered to build their own jobs and businesses." I did not expect to be confronted about my values at my first meeting with a leader of the Nickerson Gardens public housing project, Nora King, and two board members.

BOARD MEMBER: What do you get out of this? A lot of poverty pimps come here to make money off the backs of poor people.

DAVID: I was asked by residents to come here to help with strategy.

NORA: You weren't asked by me. You are going to take my story and make money with it. I know people from universities that took our story and got big grants, hundreds of thousands of dollars. We never seen none of it.

DAVID: I won't make money from this. If I do, you can have it. If I can tell your story, I can counter negative images outsiders have. I can get people involved.

NORA: Residents have learned not to trust outsiders. The professors or "poverty pimps" take surveys, conduct focus groups, provide orientation workshops, sign people up for programs. And then they get paid and the programs never do as promised. And the residents learn not to trust outsiders.

BOARD MEMBER: Professors are arrogant. They look down on the residents, use a lot of words no one understands, don't listen to us.

NORA: Residents are surrounded by experts who seem to know what's best for them: career bureaucrats at HUD [the U.S. Department of Housing and Urban Development] and elsewhere; city Housing Authority; politicians; the LAPD [Los Angeles Police Department] and Housing Authority police; professors. What makes you think you know what is best?

BOARD MEMBER: What qualifies you to tell us how to do our strategy? What is your program anyway?

NORA: Don't think we need some pink-faced person coming around here telling us how to survive in this place.

DAVID: All I know is my mother was on welfare. I know what it's like standing in line for lard and cheese. I've seen welfare workers come into my house, enter my room, pull open my drawer, and say: "Where'd you git that transistor radio? You'll have to report that as income." Listen, I was asked to come here.

My cover story is that I am just a college professor. Beneath is a story rarely shared. I switched to my deeper story.

DAVID: I grew up on welfare. I was the eldest of four children. When we were abandoned, my mother could not drive, had never worked. We came from being rich in Paris, France, to being poor in Spokane, Washington. She never accepted the divorce, turned to tranquilizers, never recovered fully. There are no projects in Spokane but pain just the same. People in a small city can be cruel, especially to poor people, to a woman without a husband, to kids without a father.

The resident leader and her board interrupted my story.

NORA: Do you believe in God?

DAVID: I do. I was an elder in my church before I got sick of the congregation's middle-class ways. Folks talked about going beyond the church walls and into the community, but they just talked.

NORA: You know God loves each and every one of us. It don't matter what color the skin is. It's what's inside that counts. We all have red blood.

DAVID: I know. I got color too. These are freckles. When I was five, I went to a neighbor's house to ask my friend to come and play.

His mother said, "Don't come in here. You are a mess. What is on your face anyway?" "Freckles," I answered. "They don't come off."

OK, having freckles is not like being Black. Being religious doesn't mean I am a good guy. But because I was on welfare and I experienced deep-seated prejudices, I have insight into economic repression.

Making Unexpected Differences
Linda Calvert

I remember one evening. The class had finally gotten comfortable talking openly about ethnicity, gender, and other issues. Students could now express personal perspectives and deal with different views and experiences without shutting down or shutting each other out. It was a moment to celebrate. However, I realized I was hearing about an "other" group—gays and lesbians as the "other." I listened. I hated to break the moment, but finally I spoke. I observed that gays and lesbians were being spoken of as if the "other," as "them." I said that I couldn't imagine in a class this size that there wasn't someone gay or lesbian and therefore we were in fact talking about us. The class fell silent. People avoided looking around. Finally, discussion picked up again, but this time with a new level of awareness.

I didn't think much about it when one student, call him David, walked out to the car with me that night. Students usually did. David was a good student who offered good insights. I noted that he had been unusually quiet tonight. After small talk, David thanked me for my sensitivity and told me how much he appreciated what I had done. He talked about his experience, partially in the closet, partially out: a white-collar worker who felt he had to be careful; a member of an ongoing work group in class where one member had made clear his conservative biases.

I listened and was moved. I remembered my own hesitancy to "break the flow" and interrupt class discussion. It would have been easy to let this one drop. I was reminded at that moment, however, that it is important to stay clear, to give voice to what is happening. It always matters. Sometimes we are privileged to know that we have made a difference. I find it strange that making a difference rarely happens in the ways I plan.

Part III

Distinctive Features of the Landscape

Part III

Distinctive Features of the Landscape

Teacher as Learner

*L*earning about diversity in all its forms is a lifelong undertaking. It is not something quickly or ever finally mastered. The more we learn, the more we realize how much there is to learn.

The topic and experience of understanding and respecting diversity are so complex, it is foolish to assume that the teacher is the ultimate, or even a major, source of knowledge. As the contributors remind us, it is common for experienced teachers and trainers to see themselves as learners. The roles of teacher and student become fluid and ultimately lose traditional meaning as all grapple with the implications of our interconnections. There is paradox inherent in all this. As teachers become learners, they model the learning process and ultimately become more effective diversity educators.

Traditional ways of teaching do not work for a subject as complex and profoundly personal as diversity. The learning is different for all. Students need to develop their own capacities for reflection, tolerance, and inquiry. Educators need to stretch their skills and understandings further and deeper. Mutual learning and constant teaching-learning interactions lead to questioning—challenging much of what we believe about the socially constructed ways we relate to one another and perpetuate systems of inequity in the workplace and beyond.

Being the Lead Learner
Barbara Walker

Diversity work delights me. It has helped me slow down and sus-
pend judgment. It has taught me to take time and pause along the
way—to reflect and make meaning of my life experiences. Ever
astute as a young student when it came to textbook knowledge, I
realize I am a slow learner about life. My "valuing differences" work
has helped me learn how to learn. As the old saying goes, "We
teach best what we're trying to learn."

Although I have had the opportunity to team-teach diversity on
a number of occasions, I do not think of my work as teaching. I do
not teach. My work is finding ways to help people learn from, about,
and across differences—whether in the classroom or in the workplace. I see myself as a lead learner who sets the tone, turns on the
lights, lights the candles, prepares the table, does anything she can
to create a safe place for learning—not teaching.

Seeing Every Interaction as Potential Learning
Duncan Spelman

Diversity teaching is challenging. Teachers need to attend simultaneously to course content and to what's happening in the moment. The
present moment is always loaded emotionally because the event is not
just one interaction with one student. Each interaction is a potential
learning experience for teacher and students: all are listening, understanding, and identifying with what's happening in different ways.

Adopting an Attitude of Learning
Myrtle Bell

In teaching about diversity, it is important not to let our personal
prejudices, stereotypes, and ignorance affect our audience or our

effectiveness. No one is enlightened about all aspects of a subject as diverse as diversity. For example, several years ago, a coworker and I traveled together often on business. We grew to know each other well. On one business trip, we talked about race and ethnicity. He was bothered by being called "Hispanic." He was Mexican and was proud to be seen as Mexican. Several years later, in a diversity course I was taking, the instructor asked people to break into groups for an experiential exercise. We were asked to self-identify as White male, White female, or person of color. In my small group, I sat next to a Hispanic man. Although he joined the persons-of-color group, it was clear from our conversation that he was not completely comfortable doing so. I wondered if his having a Hispanic surname and somewhat dark features made him feel compelled to choose the category he did despite the face that he considered himself a White Hispanic male. The man commented to me that he assumed the course instructor meant "Caucasian, non-Hispanic White male" instead of just "White male." I suggested he let the instructor know his reactions to the limited choice of categories offered.

Reflecting on all this was a tremendous diversity learning experience for me. What we do not know and are protected from learning, we continue not to know. We continue to offend. It is important to adopt an attitude of learning at all times. It is essential that we acknowledge a willingness to learn in our teaching environments, especially when we teach about diversity. In diversity work, everyone stands to learn.

Becoming More Real, Closer to Home
Peter Couch

Those of us who teach have wonderful opportunities for personal learning and development. Years ago, I began to think of myself not as a teacher but as a facilitator of learning. This reflects my experience working with adults in industry, a longtime interest in experiential learning, and the realities of teaching in an eclectic and often imprecise field like management. Presuming to be the "expert" seems inappropriate. Consequently, my approaches in the classroom involve group work, discussion, questioning, journal writing, and practical projects. These approaches create opportunities for interaction; interactions provide opportunities for teachers to learn from students both in and out of the classroom.

Working with a range of students—women and men; African-Americans, Latinos, and Whites; individuals with physical limitations, different ethnic backgrounds, sexual orientations, and more—has personalized diversity for me. One-on-one contact has led to greater empathy for and interest in other persons' problems and points of view. Recently, for example, I spent time with a student who traced his background in Mexico to the Aztecs. He had not done as well as expected in an honors class. In our discussion, I learned that he had been spending considerable time leading a group of Latino students in an "opposition rally" to communicate his feelings about the inappropriate celebration of Columbus Day. His frustration at incorrect historical interpretations of Spanish involvement in Mexico caused me to think, do some additional reading, and learn.

I recall the example of a Black student who was president of his fraternity. We had several visits about his responsibilities and problems. In one case, there had been a shooting. Some nonstudents got into an argument with students at a late-night dance on campus, got a gun, and fired several shots. One bullet hit a female student in the eye. She was blinded. The day after the shooting, my student, who did not even know the victim and whose fraternity was not directly involved, came to my office to talk about what he and his fraternity could do to help her. I gained insights into the sense of community and support among the Black students on our campus.

I also always learn from classroom diversity-oriented exercises and discussions. While some students have constructive racial attitudes, others have deep-seated biases. Their journals report racial incidents or negative family attitudes toward race. Most students, I think, are not aware of widespread, subtle discrimination. Knowing this makes me aware of what can be accomplished in classroom situations like mine where diversity issues are only a small portion of course content.

Experiences like these with students have been catalysts for further exploration into diversity issues through reading, conversations with colleagues, and experimentation. The emotional power of getting to know people who have been penalized because of their sex, race, or other differences increases my desire to learn more. The issues become more real, closer to home. I know I have become more aware of my own lack of perceptiveness and sensitivity. More than ever, learning about the problems of the disadvantaged is a matter of great personal importance to me. I have learned much in the past few years. Experiencing diversity is essential in my efforts to teach about it. It has helped me clarify my values and reinforced my commitment to help students learn from their own experiences.

Individualizing Learning: "Thanks, Steph"
Gordon Meyer

Stephanie Sayre was a member of the Bucknell University class of 1991. I was her adviser. She chose to write her senior project on diversity. We agreed that part of this project would involve conducting a structured diversity training experience for her student peers.

She chose to do this in our organizational behavior course. I became a participant in her activity. Stephanie began by putting students into same-sex groups to consider the question "What's good and bad about being male or female at Bucknell?" There were at Bucknell at the time strong feelings and tensions about gender inequalities and stereotyping. There was real potential for passion and conflict at this event.

Stephanie gently facilitated a discussion of the men's and women's lists of perceptions. Students shared some perceptions that

were probably idiosyncratic to Bucknell, but many were stereotypical, insensitive, and not unlike what one might expect in a corporate diversity training session. For instance, the men thought it must
be very good for women to have the social scene managed for them,
particularly by the male fraternities. Steph acknowledged that per-
ception and asked the women if they saw it the same way. Not surprisingly, they didn't.

It took personal courage for Steph to do this work with her
peers. It was courage that I had not shown prior to this time. I had
considered using such an exercise but had been unwilling to risk
student rejection. I feel vulnerable when challenging students in
areas where they have strongly held convictions about their own
and others' differences.

There is an important postscript to this story. Stephanie Sayre
was killed in an automobile accident a year after she graduated. The
spring after Steph died, I used her as an inspiration and a model of
how to introduce students in a human resource management course
to the issue of diversity. I used a slight variation on her exercise.
Because of time constraints, however, there was only time to share
the lists of perceptions generated by the same-sex groups. Discussion had to be postponed.

Before the next class, an outspoken male student approached. He
implored me to cancel that discussion and permit the men to apol-
ogize for some of the perceptions of women they had reported in the
previous class period—which included objectifying women as sex
objects and as inferior to men. My immediate reaction was that any
process that led a student to be that uncomfortable with what he and
his peers had done struck an important chord and shouldn't be
aborted without further exploration. My students and I explored the
meaning of the reported perceptions, the men's apology, and the
genuine resentment and pain that some women had felt in the previous class. This would not have happened without Steph as a model
of courage and a teacher willing to risk and challenge others. Thanks
again, Steph. You live on as an inspiration for me.

Teaching in a Diverse Team
Marcy Crary

There is great value in team teaching—butting up against each other's ways, styles, and inputs; struggling to work through differences and come up with a shared product at the end of our scheduled time together. It has been a rich learning medium for me.

A recent learning has been how quickly I judge others. Teaching in a diverse team (two men and two women, two white Euro-Americans and two African-Americans) forces me to recognize how I judge each member. The judgments come easily. It is more difficult to step back, look at the assumptions that underpin those judgments, and explore how they get in the way of informed action. For example, very early in one semester, two Black woman students came up to me and said that they didn't want one of the people on the teaching team to grade their papers, referring to the African-American male instructor. I said, "Fine, we can arrange that." I wanted to bond quickly with the women and was flattered that two Black women wanted a White woman like me to work with them. Wow, this is great! I overlooked this as a possible issue for my Black male colleague. Afterward, we talked about my action, and he expressed surprise at my response. We argued about appropriate next steps and eventually agreed that I should tell the students that their papers would be handled like all others—graded by two randomly determined instructors.

I could see that I had acted out of a certain blindness to the relationships at play in the situation. I chose to satisfy my own needs for inclusion and connection to the two Black women. This experience taught me early on that team teaching was a rich environment for learning about one's own perceptions, behaviors, and impact on others. Staying alert to these complexities is an ongoing challenge.

Teacher-Student
Relationships and Roles

Teacher-student relationships and roles differ in educational arenas where the teacher is also a learner. Little prepares us for this. Many of our previous educational experiences explicitly or implicitly cause both teacher and student to frame their educational roles in hierarchical terms. Traditional classroom teachers, we have been taught, have power, control, authority, and assumed knowledge. In the corporate classroom, a trainer's knowledge, understanding, and skill command even the more organizationally powerful to come, listen, and learn. Students and clients have learned through years of educational experiences how to play their expected roles. This tacit agreement between teacher and student about how teaching and learning should take place is powerful. Those who violate such agreements know the consequences all too well.

Dynamics, roles, and relationships, however, are different in diversity classrooms. As the contributors note, there is less predictability in teaching diversity than in most other subjects. Diversity issues are learned experientially, emotionally, and intellectually. Deep personal connections between teacher and students are often necessary to manage the emotional intensity that diversity teaching and learning invokes.

Classroom dynamics and group composition play a role in all teaching and learning processes. Staying aware of these dynamics, however, is even more critical in diversity education. Individuals with different "starting points" for learning—different values, lifestyles, understandings, capacities for self-reflection, willingness to accept personal complicity, experiences

with differences—bring widely disparate learning agendas to the table. Inter-
actions among multiple agendas affect the pace, intensity, and focus of the
teaching and learning. It is impossible for diversity educators to become
complacent with their courses and programs: each new configuration of
learners makes both process and content unique. Teacher or trainer and
students jointly create, struggle to understand, and manage classroom
dynamics—an exhilarating and, at times, daunting experience. As the sto-
ries of the contributors in this section vividly demonstrate, care, sensitivity,
reflexivity, and a playful spirit are essential requirements for the job.

Managing Uncertainty
Earl Avery

In diversity teaching, we ask students to deal openly with one another.
When you are in the front of a class, you never know what's really happening for people. There's uncertainty in the diversity teaching
process. If you are teaching a history course, for example, you know
there are factual data that students can give back to measure learning.
In diversity work, you don't know if, in the process of discovery, you're
going to shut people down by the way you respond to them. Should
you encourage them to say more? Allow them to work the issue inter-
nally? Student personalities and experiences are incredibly different.
As teachers, we need to deal with this uncertainty all the time.

Finding a Middle Ground
Duncan Spelman

The band within which productive conversation about differences
can occur is narrow. It's easy to collude with students: try to sound
supportive and in the process seem to agree with the content of
what people say. It's easy in the classroom when everyone agrees,
when everyone seems to get along. As the instructor, it is easier to
go along and assume that the class is moving in a productive way—

that is, until you catch your complacency and say, "Wait. There's no disagreement in this room. There's no tension."

Yet it is also easy to stir up simple conflict—confront, disagree, get into fights. People open up, but they don't have to listen to others. The process goes by too fast for learning. Issues are driven underground. It's particularly easy, I believe, to drive White men underground. It can happen without the instructor's even realizing it.

There is, however, a middle ground where powerful conversations can happen. That space is tougher to reach and manage. Individuals' emotional starting points on diversity issues tend to be anger or defensiveness, depending on which side of the issue they embrace. It is hard to establish a productive conversation between angry and defensive people.

Finding this middle ground is easier for instructors who have a "personal connection" with their class—those who feel they really know their students and whose students really know them. That connection gives instructors the freedom to play and experiment.

Altering the Usual Connections
Marcy Crary

The hardest part of team teaching is feeling as if I've lost a strong, personal connection to the class. When I taught by myself, it was "my class." Team teaching with three other people is different. As an instructor, I never have the same kind of intimacy that I do with students in my own classroom. I miss the personal ways of forging different relationships. I certainly have relationships with some students in our team-taught course, but I never feel as if I have an intuitive sense of the whole class in relationship to me. I rely on other members of the team now to tell me how students whom I don't know well are doing or what they've said in after-class conversations.

Teaching is like conducting an orchestra. When team-teaching, I feel less control of all the instruments and less clear about how my skills are contributing to the music produced. I struggle to know how well I'm doing my job. I lack the same satisfaction at the end of the term that I have when I know it's been all my work.

Acknowledging Unresolved Questions
Gordon Meyer

I am increasingly alarmed by the overtly racist and sexist attitudes in my students on topics like affirmative action and equal employment and feel impotent to deal with them. It is difficult to accept these students' distaste for affirmative action. I become enraged and despondent when I hear and read words that indicate that they have no sense of how discrimination continues to occur. A part of me wants to feel good that students are willing to be open with me. Not all believe that they have to mouth a "politically correct" line. Another part of me wants to revert to my '60s activist persona and shout down those who disagree with me.

As I ponder how I might respond, I feel vulnerable. I become concerned about being stereotyped and dismissed by my students as "politically correct." One of my Ph.D. professors described me as "too nice." He may have been right. How can I engage in learning about diversity with others while I accept them as persons but reject their expressed intolerance?

In addition to these frustrations, I'm aware of and disturbed by my observation that I'm more likely to engage in impression management when I am in the formal role of teacher than in less public settings. The impressions I present, I fear, obscure my intellectual and personal commitment to valuing diversity. I am very apprehensive about student rejection. I also too readily assume that I have to proclaim my commitment to valuing diversity in order for students to learn from it—that subtle modeling is lost. I should test both the apprehension and assumption.

Living with Little Choice but to Engage
Colleen Jones

People carry a vast array of experiences, stereotypes, and assumptions about various types of people. Many of these are not positive. I was struck by a comment from an international colleague who noted that she was surprised by the fact that I was "so American." I had to chuckle. That would be among the last phrases that I (and probably my students) would use to describe me. But there is much truth to that statement, even though it gets buried under the other labels and characterizations attached to people of color in the United States.

As an African-American female educator, students bring *two* sets of mental maps to my classes. Although the syllabus doesn't say "diversity," my classes are living laboratories about operating in and managing a diverse environment. A couple of terms ago, for example, I was teaching a graduate course in communications. I went over the organization and planning of oral presentations and explored the differences between informative and persuasive speeches. We reviewed the textbook's guidance on the subject and critiqued short paragraphs to illustrate the distinction. In my wrap-up, I used the word *obfuscate*. A snicker came from the class. A student in the back raised his hand and asked, "What did you just say?" Thinking that the summary needed clarification, I started to paraphrase my comments. Another student stopped me in mid-sentence, "No, what was that *word?*" I paused and my face obviously registered puzzlement, so a student said, "*Ob-sue?*" When I realized what I was being asked, I printed the word on the board, defined it, and went on with the summary.

During the break, a student admitted that he had gone down to the library to check *obfuscate*. I asked what he found. He reported that my spelling and explanation had been accurate. Then he asked me, "Where did you pick up that word?" I said, "Well, I read a lot," and let it pass. Inside me, Vesuvius was rumbling. My face and hands were hot. From both the comments and the students' facial expressions, it was obvious that in their frame of reference, an African-American wasn't supposed to have such a broad vocabulary. Or even worse, he believed that if it was a "big word" or sounded strange, I probably made it up to sound intelligent (as many comedy routines from Amos 'n Andy to Damon Wayans insinuate). Chalk one up for battling a stereotype without drawing my sword. Does my Momma know that is what I'm really teaching?

My presence in the classroom has the effect of freeing students to examine unfamiliar areas. Because I am familiar with feminist, African-American, and other specialty periodicals and journals, I routinely copy and distribute relevant articles from them without any fanfare about the nontraditional nature of the source. Similarly, I choose cases, scenarios, and examples that feature women, people of color, and international subjects or topics. I highlight regional differences in America, using examples and sources from the Midwest, the South, or the West Coast, given that I'm teaching in the Northeast. I just do it. However, I've discovered over the years that students learn from and respond well to this.

For example, I often ask students to select, review, and critique a scholarly article. Students turn in papers that deal with women, affirmative action, prominent African-American business people, diverse populations, and so on. The cynic inside says, "They're doing this to impress me." Another internal voice says, "Hallelujah! They're taking advantage of an opportunity and learning—*on their own*—about differences!" My infusion approach to diversity means that I work to create an environment that embraces differences, one where students are stimulated to take risks and examine their judgments and perceptions of people who appear different. Those are cherished moments as a teacher.

Creating Safe Spaces
Darlyne Bailey

My entire past and present affect my thoughts, feelings, and actions as a teacher-learner in this multidimensional area we call "diversity." Yet reality is more than diversity. To me, life is a spiritual journey of sameness *and* difference and of difference *within* sameness. We must always be mindful that not all differences are readily apparent. Sexual orientation and religious beliefs, for example, may not be immediately identifiable. As educators and trainers, our first task is to facilitate the creation of a space that is safe—free from judgment and bias and honoring of all. Only then should we encourage self-disclosure.

We must also remember to respect how others self-identify. A woman married to a man may be bisexual. A light-skinned, blond-haired, blue-eyed woman may be Latino, African-American, or Native American! In one context, a person may identify as part of the "majority" but in another situation may relate as "different" and "minority." Last year, two White students in our school's graduating class realized that their religion would not let them participate in a graduation ceremony taking place in a Jewish temple. Similarly, an individual who may appear as a "minority" to others may self-identify as a member of a more powerful group. This experience has been reported to me numerous times when Japanese students are in classes where the other Asians are Taiwanese or Korean.

Unlike the days of the '60s and '70s, being blind to another's color, class, or gender may be received as not appreciating all of who the other is. This is a tricky business, however, because that other may not want you to focus on particular aspects and would prefer that you focus on others.

Interacting with Care and Sensitivity
Myrtle Bell

My early experiences with diversity teaching make clear the importance of educating those charged as instructors and leaders. An educator's ignorance and naïveté are no longer excusable. I have spoken with Black students who were offended that professors told them they were so "articulate," asked what their parents did for a living, or assumed they were attending college on an athletic scholarship.

One Black honors student told me of having been directed to remedial English as she attempted to enroll in the Honors English course
dictated by her college entrance exam scores. The woman working
at the Honors counter looked at her and immediately said, "You
belong over there," pointing to the remedial line. As educators, we
must be sensitive to our own stereotypes and biases. We may "mean
no harm," but we damage our students and our credibility.

Integrating the Personal and Emotional into Teaching

We asked contributors to "listen to their souls and speak from their hearts" as they wrote about their diversity teaching and training experiences. We wanted this book to offer support and honest guidance to those who prepare for their own journeys. Diversity teaching requires that educators bring heart, mind, and soul to their work. There are few other teaching jobs that ask as much.

A wonderful synchronicity brought our attention to Thomas Moore's 1992 book, Care of the Soul, while we worked on this project. Moore talks about the soul as containing messy, human, contradictory, irrational, and emotional parts of the self. He emphasizes the importance of accepting and loving those parts. The parallels to diversity work are clear. Teaching workplace diversity well requires confronting the not-always-pleasant parts of one's life and being. It means bringing all of who we are to the work.

As the contributors remind us, effective diversity educators personalize that awareness. They accept their emotional responses; embrace those messy, contradictory, and irrational parts of who they are; and work to integrate all this into their teaching. They recognize that diversity teaching demands walking a fine line between focusing inside and looking out, between experiencing joy and acknowledging pain, between learning about the self and creating opportunities for others to do the same, between conceptualizing issues and sharing feelings, between acknowledging progress and staying mindful of the long road ahead. As we've heard before, the personal is the professional. The work is the journey.

Accepting the Affective Aspects of Change
Dina Comnenou

Emotional or affective work is still largely unacceptable in learning about culture. People who teach White identity development, for example, complain about the guilt Whites feel when confronted with the impact of their dominance and ethnocentrism. A more useful approach is to accept all feelings as a normal, inherent part of the change process and help people express their guilt so they can move beyond it to attitude change and action. Commonly used approaches of presenting stage theories of racial learning and expecting people to shape reactions and thinking accordingly bypass the affective aspect of change. Learning about cultures and from differences is an affective and cognitive process. We need to accept the exploration of emotions and assist students in arriving at a new integration of their thinking and feelings.

Being on the Emotional Edge
Cliff Cheng

My experience of trying to go around sadness, anger, and shame by analysis, talk therapy, or meditation has only led to more sophisticated repression. Going through the issues by feeling and processing them works better than stuffing everything deep inside me. This is *being* diversity.

Anger is a necessary part of the process. Anger is a natural human emotion in response to the continuous psychic terror of racism, sexism, classism, homophobia, religious intolerance, and other injustices. I cannot heal myself and help others until I feel my anger and work it through.

Diversity cannot be part of a heady lecture. It needs to be experienced in the body. In the West, body, emotions, mind, and spirit are split. The personal work of diversity calls for a reunion of these aspects of being. If, as an educator, I'm in my head and comfortable, I do my students, clients, and myself no good. I have to be on my edge, as uncomfortable as that is. I need to feel my anger, rage, shame, and sorrow. Without *pain*, I am unreal. I have issues in my tissues—stored emotional memory. I cannot heal without feeling and letting go of the pain.

Sharing Ourselves
Duncan Spelman

Diversity teaching requires that we share ourselves personally in the process. The more we do that, the more we get that level of reflection and self-revelation from the students.

Seeing Emotions as Essential
David Boje

My professional role and self-image are wrapped up in my personal diversity journey of self-discovery and growth. In my storytelling, I am coming to terms with my transitions from welfare recipient to professor, from poverty to middle class, and from angry rebel to system reformer.

Most welfare recipients do not grow up to be college professors. I crossed an economic and social barrier. I was the first in my family to attend college, let alone receive a Ph.D. My self is "between" my professional and working-class family roots. Though I converse with both camps, I do not feel at home at fancy academic affairs or in the welfare community.

Business education is set up to be rational and dispassionate. I try to subvert that. I invite people from the developments to audit my leadership classes at the university. I invite students to go to public housing, participate in the tutoring and adult training workshops there, do other community service projects. Students organize fundraising, set up accounting systems, and conduct environmental audits. On one occasion, we painted inner-city school classrooms. Another class did an AIDS fundraising dance and used the money to rehabilitate a shelter for mothers dying from AIDS.

These kinds of projects make learning and teaching an emotional experience. When we went to the shelter, we found that the roof needed repair. You could stick your hand through into a bedroom. It needed security lights, gardening, you name it. We raised $2,000 from the dance and used the money to do whatever we could. One weekend, we bought shrubs and flowers and constructed a meditation garden. Another weekend, we cleared the alleyway of trash and painted the alley walls. "We found a needle. No one wants to touch it. What do we do?" "Don't touch it, but scoop it up with a shovel and get on with it." These middle-class students had not seen anything like this before.

A curious thing happened. As students worked around the house and spoke to the mothers and the kids, they began to empathize with the AIDS victims. They took off the thick gloves everyone had bought so they would not actually touch something an AIDS patient had touched and stacked them in a pile in the backyard. Each workday the pile grew. Even though we knew you could not catch AIDS from touching a tub or a doorknob, people were afraid. Finally, people started to touch the AIDS patients the way people touch people in everyday life. I recall on the day of the "final exam," we all met at the shelter. Students stood in the meditation garden where the ashes of dead women were being spread and spoke about what the class had meant to them. Students and I did tearful presentations on how we overcame our own prejudices about AIDS. There were a lot of stories of overcoming resistance. Some students' parents did not want them in this part of town. The administration had initially thrown the dance off campus because we were intent on distributing condoms (it was a Catholic university). Others spoke about how their friends jumped back when they heard they went to an AIDS shelter. This is without a doubt the best class I ever taught in my life.

Uniting the Personal and the Professional
Linda Calvert

When I started teaching, I was interested in change, in making the world a better place, and in helping students become responsible corporate citizens. It always seemed to me that none of that could be taught. Nonetheless, I tried. I incorporated experience into my classes in a variety of ways—discussions, exercises, projects, and sitting in circles to process all of it. I asked students to attend to their personal knowledge and feelings as well as to books. They have kept journals and done critical incident reports. The emphasis has always been on personal knowledge and growth.

I tend to see all parts of an issue as interrelated. It never occurred to me, for example, to teach motivation in isolation from leadership or to separate either from group dynamics. I weave macro or structural topics into behavioral courses. I struggle to incorporate personal growth issues into all classes.

I remember early in my career having trouble building bridges and integrating all this. I explained my dilemma to a colleague and asked how he did it. He looked at me, quite puzzled. "If you're teaching one issue, why would you bring up these other areas?" I began to check around and found that most of my colleagues followed one text or the particular orientation of their mentor. No one questioned my assertion that one area affected another. They just didn't teach that way.

My classes, by contrast, not only required a lot of work but also asked for different kinds of thinking. I looked for ways to cushion the differences in my teaching style and expectations, but I could not change my commitments. It was a long time before I found friends and colleagues who shared my teaching perspectives and passions.

Meanwhile, I was growing and changing. I participated in various National Training Lab workshops on group dynamics, watched

Carl Rogers in his workshop on conflict resolution with diverse populations, and immersed myself in various types of psychologically oriented training. I did what one would consider my "personal work." One '60s-flavored line stayed with me for years: "The most radical political act is self-transformation." I played with what that meant while my involvement in all kinds of service work in the university and professional organizations gave me opportunities to observe and work with other people.

I saw how much the personal and emotional lives of people around me influenced who they were and what they did—how they taught, acted as administrators, and behaved in meetings and in the halls. I could see that often people did not see the limitations of their own frames of reference, personal experiences, and social contexts. I noticed the ways in which dominant group members assumed that everyone else saw the world as they did or, if not, "they should." I still struggled with how to incorporate the personal with the professional and the organizational, especially in my teaching.

During this time, the dean asked me to put together a women in management seminar with a male colleague. I enjoyed the experience and learned. I started teaching women in organizations courses on a regular basis. I had always done group dynamics exercises and other experientially oriented projects in my organizational behavior classes. It was in the women in organizations classes, however, where I began to see clearly the importance of systematically incorporating the personal and the emotional and exploring the implications of both. My reading of the women's literature supported my choices.

As I continued to read, listen, and teach, I began to understand more fully my refusal to deny my own experience, my need to claim my reality, my passion to unite the personal and the professional. My personal and emotional histories are who I am. I am deeply affected by the culture that surrounds me. Structural biases and personal prejudices of all kinds shape my relationship to myself and others. In many ways, my passion for teaching women's classes emerged from the conflicts I saw between what I experienced in organizations and what I saw and taught as possible for myself, others, and organizations. Like everyone who teaches, I bring what I have to my teaching—who I am and what I know.

Institutional, Structural, and Systemic Issues

*D*iversity teaching requires more than attention to intrapersonal and interpersonal concerns. It demands an equal focus on the structural and institutional issues that create and maintain inequity. These systemic issues play out in a number of ways. A school or corporation's "position on diversity," for example, affects the context for teaching and learning. Institutions provide encouragement and real incentives for teacher and students alike to undertake this difficult work—or send implicit messages that "lip service" is sufficient. On an instructional level, educators need keen awareness of systemic issues and ways of enabling learners to translate their "personal insights" into policies and practices for institutional change.

The contributors in this section make us aware that structural, institutional, and systemic forces are potent sources of pain and discrimination. They can be more difficult to identify than individual or interpersonal issues—more distant and abstract, difficult to untangle, and harder to get a clear handle on. The power of institutional and structural forces may even be magnified by the reality that it is hard for a single individual to change entrenched systems.

Institutional, Structural, and Systemic Discrimination
Linda Calvert

Over the years, I have been powerfully affected by institutional, structural, and systemic issues. I have also seen too many other women struggling to figure out "what they did wrong" when the answers were systemic as well as personal. I find it interesting when male colleagues check in with me because of my understanding of the political system—their political system—which I must understand to survive. I've had to come to terms with my own powerlessness to make people more conscious of systems.

Lack of Institutional and Societal Support
Dina Comnenou

I find it painful not being able to transmit my excitement and captivation with cultural transition to students because of external factors affecting my teaching, research, and courses. In academia, one lives with others' perceptions, definitions of "appropriate" methodologies, and research limitations due to biases about what constitutes acceptable data. When I am able to transcend these institutional and social barriers, I make meaningful connections with my students. If limited by them, I deprive my students and myself of valuable knowledge and experiences. Being a change agent in the field of multiculturalism often results in a struggle to communicate the complexities and profound changes inherent in this work. Although challenging, the successful outcomes of these efforts are highly rewarding.

The Interpersonal: Necessary but Insufficient
Gordon Meyer

One of my regrets is that my actions emphasize interpersonal interventions in dealing with diversity issues, not active confrontations of systemic or institutional issues that inhibit growth and opportunity for individuals perceived as different. At times, I have thought that interpersonal exchanges were sufficient. I am too easily reminded, however, that there are structural issues that concerned persons must be willing to confront in order for real progress to occur.

The Harm of Words Without Action
Myrtle Bell

Institutional support for diversity programs and intolerance for discrimination and prejudice are critical for behavioral and attitudinal change. Institutional support must be visible and believable. Words without action do more harm than no words at all.

I had firsthand experience of the importance of institutional support in 1977 when I headed off to college at Notre Dame. I was a young Black Protestant from the South headed to the home of the predominantly White Catholic "fighting Irish" in the Midwest. At that time, about 3 percent of the Notre Dame students were Protestant and less than 2 percent were Black. The environment was homogeneous and ripe for diversity learning.

Like many freshmen, my roommate and I corresponded during the summer, making plans to decorate, shop, and enjoy our freshman year together. She and her parents got to the room first. When my family and I arrived, she exclaimed, "She's colored!" and promptly left the room to request a room change. After my initial shock, I was amused that she said "colored." The rector of the dormitory refused to let her change rooms. Her alternative was to move off campus. Her behavior was inconsistent with Notre Dame's institutional beliefs and policies. Policy, not attitude change, prevented her from acting on her desire to move out. In addition to teaching my roommate a lesson, the rector's decision taught me about the need for institutions to stand up for what they purport to believe.

Many organizations, however, do not relay the importance of diversity to their employees. I have spoken with numerous individuals who know of managers who fail to "value" diversity in their organizations, sometimes naively, other times overtly, yet suffer no consequences even in organizations that ostensibly promote valuing diversity. The consensus from entry-level employees to high-level managers with whom I have spoken is that to effect change, demonstrated institutional support beyond diversity training, buttons, teams, and slogans is vital. Demonstrated support should include managers being measured and rewarded or punished for their diversity progress. Who are the highest-level persons in the organization? What are their educational and experience levels? What key or leadership roles do diverse people occupy? What is the distribution of awards and promotions in their organization? How do persons of color in the organization feel about their opportunities? Extra care must be taken to ensure that managers are discouraged from distorting the truth. They must understand their personal stake in valuing diversity for the corporation. They must recognize the business *and* personal consequences of not doing so.

In the week before I began to write this piece, I attended a diversity workshop, conducted to educate people in my work organization about the importance of valuing diversity. It was attended by the entire finance and planning organization—thirty-five people. I was pleased at the timing. It would give me the opportunity to observe others being taught and learning about workplace diversity and formulate thoughts for this piece. Even so, I went to the workshop with a skeptical mind. I know that talk is cheap.

One of the sections of the workshop included videos of race and sex discrimination against carefully selected and otherwise equal people. In the videos, a young Black man was told that all apartments were rented, yet when a young White man went to the same place later that day, he was shown a unit; a young White woman was steered to a secretarial job and given a typing test, whereas a young White man at the same office on the same day was encouraged to apply for a managerial position.

After the videos, the facilitator asked participants if we felt that differential treatment occurred in our organization. I knew my opinion but remained silent. Tentatively, one participant noted that there was only one Black person (me) in the organization and that something must therefore be amiss. As everyone, slightly uncomfortable, looked my way, I nodded, knowing that in this kind of situation, someone else's statement carried more weight than mine.

Another participant noted the negative impact of perceptions of a glass ceiling in the workplace. He said to imagine that half the workforce, the White males, think that regardless of their performance, they will get the best jobs, promotions, and raises, while the other half (White females and men and women of color) think that no matter how hard they work, the White males will get the best jobs, promotions, and raises. Neither group would be motivated to perform to the best of their ability, and the company would suffer for it. As a group of finance personnel, the bottom-line impact of failing to value a large portion of the workforce became clearer to us all.

Our Preference for Easier Questions
Jean Ramsey

Students in the classes I teach at Texas Southern always remind me of the ways in which I don't see structural and systemic issues. In a graduate class in organization theory, for example, we were talking about the "core groups" and "valuing differences" work at Digital Equipment Corporation. The students were impressed, as most are, with the personal and interpersonal implications of this work. What they most wanted to know, however, was the outcomes. How many persons of color were there in top management now? Has that changed as a result of the "valuing differences" program? When layoffs occurred, what proportion of men and women of color are laid off as compared to White women and men? Though I have read reports of the work at Digital, I have never seen those statistics. I have no data to support my assumption—and hope—that this work at the individual and group levels has had some effect on the way in which the organization conducts its business.

I've always been clear on the concept of institutionalized sexism since, as a White woman, I have experienced it. One reading of

Anne Wilson Schaef's book (1981) immediately sensitized me to its invasiveness and pervasiveness in my present and past organizational experiences. Understanding institutionalized racism is more difficult for me. I have searched diversity books and found little that addresses institutional and systemic issues. Taylor Cox's work (1993) was the first to make some institutional issues explicit. For example, he talks of the ways in which performance appraisal systems contain assumptions about appearance, speech patterns, demeanor, dress, and interpersonal and communication styles that systematically discriminate against members of some groups. My real understanding—an understanding that goes beyond a victimization perspective—comes from sources that normally lie outside the range of a traditional management professor—Third World feminist literature, Black studies, and fiction by persons of color.

I am now beginning to question the ways in which my teaching and the structure of my classes perpetuate forms of discrimination and inequity. In what ways, for example, does a focus on abstract conceptualization and critique systematically exclude and devalue those who learn best through active experimentation or visual imagery? In what ways has our emphasis on conformity—starting and ending classes at certain times, making uniform assignments to everyone, assuming that the "best" students are the most verbally active, rewarding the "right answers"—re-created and reinforced institutionalized isms? How do we value everyone in the classroom, whatever their group memberships or particular ways of being or learning? How do the structure and activities of classes—classes on diversity or on any topic—reinforce existing power inequalities or reinscribe new ones? My self-interrogation on these kinds of institutional diversity issues has just begun. Is it any wonder that we prefer to ask easier questions?

Dilemmas and Paradoxes in the
Teaching-Learning Process

A continuing theme in the book is the complexity of the diversity teaching and learning process. The personal and professional challenges of the work, the need for ongoing learning, the emotion-filled nature of the teaching, the nontraditional teacher and student roles, the evolving nature of the field, the different starting points and learning agendas, the distinctive personalities and developmental capacities of teacher and student, and the unpredictability of the work combine to make for twists and turns along the educational route.

Diversity work demands an openness to deep learning, an ability to accept multiple perspectives on reality, and a tolerance for exploring the often unexamined parts of human experience—areas blocked by fear, guilt, embarrassment, and denial. Defenses are easy to evoke as individuals look at themselves in ways that often stand in contrast to their espoused definitions of self. Educators wonder if and what students learn. Students question educational methods and their own capacities for growth. The work is filled with dilemmas and paradoxes.

True diversity learning, for example, demands both an immersion in confusion and increased clarity about self and others. It requires simultaneously holding on to core beliefs while letting go of rigid self-concepts and worldviews. It means that educators must model the pain and struggles in learning while concurrently conveying the confidence and professionalism students require to feel safe and open to learning. It requires holding onto *differences and similarities at the same time. It means staying in the moment without losing sight of the big picture, emphasizing emotions without ignoring cognitive clarity, sharing diversity experiences without speaking for all members of a particular group, and surfacing stereotypes and misperceptions without reinforcing them in the process.*

The experiences of the contributors demonstrate that there are no simple answers or solutions to the paradoxes and dilemmas implicit in diversity education. Making the implicit explicit, however, enables both teacher and student to navigate the diversity terrain with greater ease.

Holding On and Staying Open
Barbara Walker

In dialogue groups, participants will question whether the valuing differences philosophy has meaning beyond the workplace—whether it applies to the deeply disturbing issues raised by differences in world values. They ask, if valuing differences means accepting all people as they are, where do you draw the line?

This is a relatively easy question to deal with at the organizational level. Organizations have boundaries. Boundaries mean that organizations can establish their own core values and principles. In effect, these core beliefs "draw the line" for the organization and establish bottom-line behaviors expected of all employees. This is organizational sameness.

At the personal level, however, the question is more difficult. It raises a paradox. Diversity work means that each participant has two simultaneous tasks: developing and holding on to one's own private values while at the same time staying open to learning about and from the differences of others. The challenge is keeping these two polarities—holding on and staying open—in optimum balance. Learning to value differences is a process of constant adjustment as each of us seeks an authentic, personal point of balance.

Appreciating Everyone
Marcy Crary

I'll never forget the White student who wrote at the end of his final paper, "I hated this course more than any other course I've ever taken." When I read that, my heart sank. But as I read on, I began to smile. The student wrote about how he was raised on his grandfather's racism and how deeply the course challenged a core part of him.

All this, however, got me thinking about how different students come to this work. How well do I teach them from wherever they choose to begin their learning? How well do I appreciate them at all stages of discovery? know where they need to go on this learning journey? ask the questions that get them moving along? I need a better map about student development on these issues: to know where an individual might be and how we as educators might better help that person learn.

In diversity teaching, we really don't know how students are taking the material and what's really going on inside them. The learning process is so emotional and personal. We can't easily use objective questions, multiple-choice tests, or problem sets to know whether students are learning or not. "Getting it" is an ongoing process in diversity learning. It is hard to know how effective we, as educators, are in the whole process.

Managing Perceptual Mismatches
Colleen Jones

As an instructor, I have been bathed in the waters of "facilitate, don't preach." Create open environments, narrow distance between people, level status. That intuitively fits for me and works well for most Euro-American and international male professors. In conversations with many women faculty, however, I find that the theory doesn't exactly pan out for us. In my graduate organizational behavior course, I've adopted the practice of having students make a weekly written evaluation of each class. I ask them to comment on "content, concepts, class, and professor."

One semester, about three weeks into the term, the day's topic was personality assessment. I "lectured" on the interpretation of an assessment instrument. This was the first "talking head" presentation I'd done that semester. There were few questions. Body language shouted "unengaged" and "bored."

Later that evening, I read the students' evaluations. To my amazement, I saw comments like, "Finally, a real M.B.A. class. We heard from the teacher!" "I wish we could get more lectures." "Tonight, you worked for a change." Although these don't represent the tone of all the comments, they do indicate that what had been happening in class prior to that night was not what many students expected. I hadn't met their expectations of "teacher." Do I sermonize from the pulpit of organizational behavior (OB) wisdom and get great teaching evaluations, or do I follow the OB group process learning organization credo and have students feel that they are teaching themselves? Where's the happy medium?

How much of this perceptual mismatch can be attributed to race, gender, or simply passive students? It is hard to say. I do know, however, that the further I diverge from students' expectations of what should go on in the classroom, the more I run the risk of causing cognitive dissonance that might interfere with student achievement and development of managerial competencies and skills.

Staying with the Dialogue While Not Speaking for All
Earl Avery

People have difficulty discussing racial issues with someone of a different race. When incidents occur, such as those involving Rodney King or O. J. Simpson, most people do not have the opportunity to exchange ideas in a useful forum. Instead they have TV commentators, movie stars, or other media personalities give them answers. This is not dialogue.

When students come to class after public race-related events, they want to have a discussion. The dilemma is finding ways of communicating what I believe to be the feelings of the Black community while making students understand that I do not speak for all Black folks. I am one Black person who has a point of view about what occurred.

I can't speak for all Blacks. I can't even speak for my family: we all differ on these issues. I think the tendency for many Whites is to think, "OK, I have someone here I know," and then take that one person's opinion as gospel. It forces me regularly to make statements that I can't and won't speak for other folks. I then try to present the range of attitudes prevalent in the Black community around a particular issue in such a way that people understand that there isn't some monolithic group called "Black folks."

Addressing Oppression Without Adding to It
Marcy Crary

We often deal with powerful issues in the diversity classroom. Staying awake to potential dominant versus nondominant group dynamics can be a difficult challenge. We are all implicated in these moments by our own group identities. When we do sessions on race socialization where we ask people to think back to the race messages they received as children, we feel tension about whether or not we are putting students of color in unnecessary pain for the sake of learning for the White people in the room. How do we not disadvantage the women and people of color while addressing the realities of oppression in organizations and society? Do we risk reinforcing stereotypes by putting them out there once again for all to witness? We have worked on ways to address these concerns in our classroom. Somehow the questions still hang in my consciousness.

Unlearning Critical Assumptions
Gordon Meyer

As a diversity teacher, the present leg of my journey is a significant climb. My fear of rejection by students and colleagues is a significant barrier to taking interpersonal risks and being fully present. I assume that effective diversity teachers have less need to be liked by their students than I do. Jean Ramsey's response to my assumption, however, was instructive and provocative for me. She said that it was terribly important to her that students like her, but she has come to understand that the fear of rejection is often based in wrongheaded assumptions about what leads to such rejection. My journey has me unlearning old assumptions and replacing them with different beliefs about how students come to like and appreciate their teachers.

Living on the Margin
Cliff Cheng

Living on the margin, not being an American while living and working in America as an ethnographer and change agent, enables me to have a different view of the center, of Euro-Americans, and of people trying to be Euro-American.

One of the paradoxes of being a diverse person is that I'm seen as one-dimensional. Conservatives see me as just a teacher of the "soft" diversity stuff that White men in power fund because it's politically correct. Liberals see a stereotype that they can patronize and pity to assuage guilt for their own privilege.

There is also paradox in being a marginalized academic. Euro-Americans pass me by in their hectic competitive pace. I speak, think, and feel too slowly to catch up to them, let alone have conversations or friendships. They ethnocentrically judge me as stoic and exclude me from their social and cultural lives. So as not to feel the pain, I retreat into my head. I "go academic" on them and live in my head where they can't get in to hurt me. Pretty soon the stoic label fits. It is like quicksand. I can't get out.

Being Seen Unidimensionally
Dina Comnenou

Diversity educators can be stereotyped by our choice of professional interests. We are often seen as troublemakers, radicals, people who cannot fit or thrive in the mainstream. Rarely are we seen as experts in an important area. I have worked as an organization development specialist, therapist, manager, and educator. Until I began focusing more directly on issues of diversity, I was never seen in a negative light. Now I've become suspect. My research is suddenly seen as less valuable and less sound; my academic abilities, less impressive. Prior to the shift, I was seen as a professional with several specializations. Now colleagues respond as if I have no skills other than advocating for diversity, and they question the validity of this focus. I am mostly invited to converse and teach about diversity-related issues, not other subjects. It is as if knowing about multiculturalism strips me of other areas of expertise. My skills and knowledge are increasingly marginalized as I become a stronger, more empowered advocate of cultural pluralism.

In reality, the multicultural dimension of my work informs, expands, and deepens my skills and knowledge in other areas. I am certain that the marginalization that many of us experience is part of the struggle, part of the journey to cultural pluralism in the institutions in which we live and work.

Acknowledging Both Differences and Similarities
Jean Ramsey

A dilemma for me, as a White woman working and teaching in a predominantly Black environment, is how much attention to pay to issues of race. On the one hand, they are absolutely unavoidable when talking about organizational and management issues. The organizational experiences of African-Americans are not the same as those of their White counterparts. There's no use pretending otherwise. On the other hand, everything cannot be attributed to race. This ignores the complexities and realities of our multiple identities. It makes the danger of "victimizing" ever present. If Black women writers have taught me anything, they have taught me the meaning of agency.

In the classroom, then, as we struggle with issues of diversity, I am often torn over how much to focus on differences, how much on similarities. One alternative is transcendence—searching for ways to "rise above" our differences. Holding the belief that "underneath, we're all the same" can have the effect of trivializing real, lived experiences. Similarly, equating all differences can leave individuals feeling devalued. I am reminded of a class where we discussed corporate diversity training efforts. One woman described the diversity efforts of the major corporation for which she worked. The corporation required everyone to attend diversity training workshops, but in the one she attended, every time someone brought up an issue of race, it was translated into, countered with, or compared to issues of gender. You can imagine how "valued" she, as an African-American woman, felt. The message was clear: "we're willing to talk about the female part of you but not the African-American part."

Reading a poem by Pat Parker, called "To the white person who wants to know how to be my friend," helped me understand that it is not an either-or question. In the poem, Parker tells us that the first thing a White person needs to do is to forget that an individual is Black. She is quick to add, however, that the second thing is to never forget that that individual is Black (Parker, 1978, p. 68). Therein lies the paradox. I must learn to hold both views simultaneously. I must ever be cognizant of differences, the ways in which our experiences have been distinctly shaped by our group memberships. I must not assume that everyone has the same view of the world, the same set of expectations and assumptions, the same lived experiences. Yet I must also search for the similarities. There are likely more of them than differences if we can just get to them. Similarities and differences have to be constantly held up for public view and interrogation. That's not an easy task.

Honoring Multiple Selves
Darlyne Bailey

The challenge educators face is to remember that all people are multicultured and therefore embody multiple selves. In diversity classes and in all arenas where teaching and learning are valued, if we want truly to honor all, we must invest time and use both head and heart to discover in self and other how we all want to be known. We must remember that each of our lives is a magic story needing to be told. To teach, preach, research, or even consult about diversity is to educate self and other about the divine interconnections in life, the polycultural ties that bind.

Team Teaching

Many diversity educators work alone. Corporate training budgets in an era of retrenchment and university teaching load requirements and policies often make it difficult to justify multiple faculty for a single course or program. All we know about the demands and complexities of teaching workplace diversity, however, make choices for solitary teachers or trainers seem penny-wise and pound-foolish.

Three of the contributors to this book, Earl Avery, Marcy Crary, and Duncan Spelman, regularly team-teach a diversity course at Bentley College in Waltham, Massachusetts. Their experiences speak to the unique benefits of a diverse teaching team and of having others to use as learning foils and mirrors. From their work together, members of the team learn firsthand and in "real time" about diversity, the challenges of the teaching and learning process, one another, and themselves. They feel supported in their learning and develop increased confidence in their abilities to provide varied and safe opportunities for student learning. Teaching in a heterogeneous team leads to a "natural diversity curriculum" for teacher and students as issues of similarity and difference play themselves out in day-to-day team interactions and choices.

A Natural Diversity Curriculum
Marcy Crary

From its conception, this course has been a source of personal and professional development. I use it as one way of learning about issues of difference.

Our own work as a diverse team has included the need to manage different levels of experience and styles; competing paradigms for diversity work; different levels of closeness between members; different organizational identities as faculty, administrators, and consultants; different ways of conceptualizing the centrality of academic teaching in our lives. Managing these differences has led to the need for ongoing support, feedback, constructive confrontation, sensitivity to inclusion and exclusion issues, openness, and honesty.

Looking back at the variety of issues we have explored in our team work, I find things like these:

- Exploring and acknowledging our own developmental work in responding to teachable moments in the classroom

- Writing and presenting at a national teaching conference a case about Marcy's response to, and team issues that arose from, two Black students' request that Earl not grade their papers

- Examining how we work to "complexify" students' mental maps of diversity issues and how the evaluation of their maps interacts with our own on student development issues

- Exploring class dynamics and responses when men are in the minority in a diversity course

- Discussing what it means to teach "developmentally" on diversity issues and the implications for classroom conditions

I can easily see the richness of the "natural curriculum" that evolves out of our team work on diversity learning. We have opportunities to engage in exploring intrapersonal, interpersonal, group, intergroup, and organizational issues.

Important Learnings
Earl Avery

I've learned important things about myself in this team-teaching process. One has to do with gaining a better understanding of the complexities of the work. I come to diversity teaching from involvement in the civil rights movement. There I learned to put people in categories—good guys, bad guys—and to deal with them accordingly. It was an easy way to look at and work with differences. Our teaching together has helped me understand that diversity work is far more complex.

I've also learned that I have a natural resistance to conservative theories and ideas that crop up. I can still easily put people into one of my "civil rights days" categories when, for example, students present what I see as half the picture. I try to deal with my resistance around all that.

A third critical learning for me is a new consciousness in dealing with students. I constantly examine my own behavior and look at how I interact with students, particularly White students. I don't want to do things that will hold off dialogue. Do I, for example, take a certain position that may be radical but, from that point on in the course, results in losing opportunities to engage students? Or do I take a different path and keep doors open for later communication? For me, weighing the consequences of my teaching choices has been an important learning.

Ambiguity and Uncertainty
Marcy Crary

In team-teaching the diversity course, I often feel slightly off balance. In the process of trying to choreograph our work together, I regularly ask, "What role should I be playing? Am I present enough? Do I disappear when we talk about gender socialization?" and so on. I wonder where I am with other team members. Are they OK with how things are going, with my role, with their roles? Are we being inclusive as a team, maximizing each of our styles and strengths, or do we unconsciously play out traditional roles of gender and race? In essence, the process of team teaching creates another subtext or curriculum for our own work. That curriculum has its own accompanying layers of ambiguity and uncertainty. This can be stimulating, rewarding, and exasperating.

Clarification of One's Thinking
Earl Avery

I know I get a better feel for the other teaching team members and sort through my own thinking when we do our grading together. Some of our best discussions have been after I have written a comment, we exchange papers, and Marcy, for example, asks, "Why did you interpret this instance in this way?" We talk and agree or perhaps agree to disagree. That's been an important part of the teamwork.

Alternative Approaches
Duncan Spelman

From our teaching team, I've learned that I often assume that a style difference is a quality difference. When we talk about the best way to handle an incident in the classroom, for example, I can begin the conversation with a tacit assumption that there's one way to do things and that a person may be better or worse on that dimension. This is different from beginning our discussions believing that there is a range of different approaches and styles that are equally valid—maybe not equally effective, but at least equally

valid to be considered and discussed. People have different capacities and styles. Men and women, for example, can approach issues
of structure, control, authority, and all kinds of things differently.
I probably would not have learned about all that as quickly had I
not been team-teaching.

Other Ways of Teaching

*M*ost people agree that effective diversity education is experiential in the broadest sense of the word. Teaching and learning are not limited to formal classrooms or training centers. Much comes through interacting and interconnecting with diverse others in mutually satisfying and growth-enhancing ways. As the contributors remind us, teaching opportunities come unexpectedly, even unintentionally. They arise naturally through interactions and behavior. They can occur simply through being and doing oneself in a way that values others.

Teaching Through Being
Myrtle Bell

In my junior high and high school years, I attended University High, a predominantly White laboratory school on the campus of Louisiana State University in Baton Rouge. For six years, I was one of two Blacks in a class of sixty. In my second year at U-High, as we called it, I took a Louisiana history class, and the young, White student teacher, a woman from the southern part of Louisiana, kept referring to Blacks as "Nigras." After several minutes of the lecture, I decided I would correct her after class, which I did. She said that "Nigras" was all she had ever used but that she had meant no harm by it. She was not pleased about my comments. As a twelve-year-old student, I was teaching the teacher.

I also noticed early in my tenure at U-High that the students called the custodians (all Black, as I recall) by their first names, rather than referring to them as "sir" or "ma'am" as they did the other adults at school. There were two custodians whom I remember, a middle-aged Black woman, Mandy, and a middle-aged Black man, Solomon. I made a point to ask Mandy and Solomon their last names and called them Mr. and Mrs. When other students said Mandy had said thus and so, I would ask if they meant Mrs. So-and-So. In a way, I was teaching.

For some of the students, I was the first Black person they knew other than their "maids." When I first got to U-High, several of the students asked me if I knew their maid. I always asked the maid's full name (which they often did not know) and replied as such when I did not know her. After a while, I began telling them that there were a lot of Black people in Baton Rouge and that we did not all know each other.

As I am teaching now, I have daily opportunities to explore diversity regardless of the stated class objectives. In one class this fall, one of the topics was equal employment opportunity. Many of the discussion points were discrimination in employment, sex and race segregation of jobs, and similar issues. After class, a White male student tentatively asked where I was from: he wondered if I had been raised in the "inner city." I told him I was from Baton Rouge and that there may have been no "inner city" there. He said he'd seen a television program about Blacks in inner cities being taught about corporate America, in an effort to help make them more competitive for jobs. He suggested that because some Blacks do not speak well, that, rather than their race, might be impeding their progress in organizations. As I probed, he stated that some Blacks, for example, say "ax" instead of "ask." I noted that I am Black but don't say "ax." I then said that many of our notions about what's right and proper in organizations may be based on stereotypes rather than actuality and what's really important. Another lingering student (a White female) at that point agreed and noted that the

Texan spoken by many Texas Whites receives far less focus but is neither correct nor pleasing to the ear. She provided a particularly good, nearly unintelligible example. We laughed and left, enlightened. I was pleased that students felt comfortable enough to be candid in their comments and that I was confident enough not to be angry and defensive in mine. Such lessons are not part of the curriculum but may ultimately be more important than many things we study formally.

When I began the switch from corporate employee to full-time academic, one goal was to touch students' lives. Particularly important was to touch Black students' lives, possibly in a historically Black institution. But then an adviser pointed out how many Black, White, and other lives I could touch at a predominantly White school instead. He noted that students at predominantly Black schools often have good faculty role models of color, whereas students of all racial and ethnic backgrounds at predominantly White schools have few, if any, Black female professors. He noted that my mere presence would be a lesson to some and an encouragement and a role model to others. Sometimes there is teaching simply through being.

Doing Oneself in Ways That Value Others
Gordon Meyer

I'm increasingly aware of my relative comfort in "doing myself" in a way that is sensitive to difference and communicates a willingness to deal with it directly. My best diversity work, I think, has occurred in settings that I don't think of as teaching settings.

As my graduation from Brigham Young University approached, for example, I was invited to participate in the Graduate School of Management convocation. Being different and learning about a different culture had been so central to my Brigham Young experience that I immediately thought that a natural topic for my address, even though it felt risky.

I have vivid memories of delivering the address. In an overflowing auditorium occupied by graduates and their families, I began to speak in a quivering voice. I was frightened. I opened by saying that I hoped my comments reflected the commitment to thought combined with the heartfelt sentiment captured in the words of a singer-songwriter friend: "All through my life I've tried to know things from deep inside; not just learning in my head, but feeling what I know." I noted the personal nature of my comments and several features of the Brigham Young environment that I had come to value. My most pointed remarks, however, were critical of the institutional culture.

I gave examples of assumptions that my wife must be a Mormon, since I wasn't but was attending school here. I noted the tendency to "explain" differences as a result of not being a member of "the Church," dismissing my own beliefs as unimportant. I added: "The tendency to explain one's difference in terms of any simplistic category is a dangerous one for all involved. On the part of the person who categorizes, it implies a lack of rigor in encountering and understanding others, and for me, the individual who has been categorized, it provides a potential cop-out, making it easy to justify my value position and actions only in terms of fitting into a category. I do not respect such a lack of rigor in myself or others."

There were gratifying acknowledgments of my comments from students and a female faculty member who called my address "a fine moment." But probably most important to me were the words of the other student who addressed the convocation. When I returned to my seat, she thanked me and said she wished she could have said the things I did. I am proud that I can stand tall and "do myself" in ways that express valuing others for their uniqueness.

Walking Our Talk
Duncan Spelman

I wonder about the impact of our choices as a racially and sexually diverse teaching team on students and their learning. As colleagues, we know the reality of full-time versus part-time status, outside commitments, team agreements, different skills and interests, and so on. We understand the dynamics and choices going on, but how do students see it all from the outside? Do students say, for example, "Look, the Black woman misses more classes" or "The White man is up front much more"? At the beginning of the course, we tell students we are four equals. To some extent we are; in other ways we are not. If students are holding us to the same standards and expectations, we may be sending messages other than the ones we intend.

We tend to spend our time together as a team tending to the mechanics of teaching—who's going to do the next class, how we will grade, and the like. These are important issues, but the interesting thing from my perspective is that when we have time, we choose to talk about diversity issues in non-team-related ways. We have fascinating and stimulating conversations. But we don't spend much time on our dynamics as a team: how we work together, what our differences bring, and so on. We don't work our own issues around race, gender, part-time versus full-time status, or different backgrounds or styles or skills.

I know it is easier to avoid those tough issues. But that means we don't always "walk our talk" as a group: we're not doing what we tell our students to do. Under the supposed pressures of time, we leave critical issues about our differences and their impact on the team unworked. I worry about what we then unknowingly teach our students.

Why is it so hard for us to do that work? Answering that question is important. The nonuniversity work world has even more pressures for people to get a project done. Like us, when diversity issues come up, those folks will probably ignore them and focus on getting the assigned job done.

Part IV

Seeing the Journey as the Work

Vulnerability

*I*n this day and age, unless one belongs to an extreme social group, it is impo-
lite—even "politically incorrect"—to admit prejudice against members of
groups different from one's own. We know, however, that the world is far from
bias-free. Many who espouse openness to and acceptance of difference admit
otherwise in private moments and unintended slips. Others cling to definitions
of themselves as nonprejudiced even though their thoughts, behaviors, and reactions contradict those self-concepts. Human inconsistencies make the vulnerability essential for effective diversity teaching and learning difficult.

As theorists like Chris Argyris and Don Schön (1974) remind us, we
all hold espoused beliefs about ourselves consistent with our governing
values—values we have learned as important from family and experience, values we believe all "good" people hold. Yet while we adamantly
adhere to beliefs about ourselves as "good" individuals, we may be unable
to live up to our own expectations. At the same time, it is too painful to
admit the gap. We therefore espouse one thing to ourselves and others yet
do another. We remain oblivious to any discrepancy. It's not conscious
deception. It's common human behavior.

In the context of teaching and learning about workplace diversity,
this is troublesome. It is as if something deep within us is "programmed"
to collude with our inability or refusal to explore not-so-pleasant beliefs
about and reactions to people seen as different from ourselves. Even the
best and most open of us carry biases, stereotypes, and unproductive
expectations about others we've learned from our childhood, education,

and life experiences in a complex society. We have to work hard to acknowledge the prejudices, intolerance, and unacknowledged assumptions we secretly wish we did not carry.

There is no hiding, however, in effective diversity education. Deep emotion, hidden fears, and tacit assumptions are all grist for the teaching-learning mill. Diversity work requires a recognition that we all, no matter what our group membership, regularly engage in racism, sexism, and every other kind of ism that exists. This admission bares the soul. It pushes against our powerful, self-protecting, psychological defense mechanisms. It asks us to hold up our values, beliefs, and behaviors for scrutiny in the name of learning. It makes us vulnerable to ourselves and others.

Add to this the usual feelings of vulnerability all educators bring to a complex educational table, and it is no surprise that even the most experienced diversity educators feel continuously vulnerable in their teaching roles. Their vulnerabilities, as the contributors who speak in this section tell us, come from multiple sources and play themselves out in many forms.

Questions About One's Capabilities
Marcy Crary

I feel vulnerable when working with diversity learning. This vulnerability comes in many forms. I carry, for better or worse, an ongoing sense that I don't know enough, may not be "good enough," and may not be prepared to respond adequately to the "next critical moment" in the class. I frequently question my own and others' effectiveness in doing this work. I'm often working to contain my own anxieties and tensions about how well we are connecting and responding to individual students, given where they are on the issues.

Vulnerability as New Territory for White Males
Gordon Meyer

As I write, I am in the midst of difficult personal and professional transitions. I am in the first year of a new teaching position at a new

institution that is different from my previous one. I didn't leave
Bucknell of my own accord; in fact, it had become a comfortable
and exciting professional home. My departure from Bucknell was,
in some ways, made more difficult by the fact that I had close colleagues there who also regretted my going.

I am lonely at my new institution and in my new community.
Although such loneliness is expected, it is nonetheless painful and
a source of vulnerability. I wonder if my vulnerability might be a
source of transformational teaching. Is it possible that feeling
exposed, with one's emotions so close to the surface, makes the self-
disclosure, genuineness, and empathy that are essential to the diversity teaching and learning journey easier? Or does vulnerability
reduce my willingness to take the risks necessary to teach and learn
about differences?

My initial judgment is that my vulnerability has not been a
source of greater openness with students. I have relied heavily on
close friends and family for support. My students aren't friends at
that level, and openness with them about my personal issues doesn't
feel safe—and probably shouldn't. At least I don't think it appropriate to use students as sources of that kind of support. Yet being
very much aware of one's feelings and need for such support might
make one more open, more fully present, and in those ways more
human in the classroom. I don't think that's been the effect for me.

I wonder if these are questions that only a White male who
benefits from the privileges associated with that status is likely to
ask. White male status makes vulnerability unnecessary in some
sense. It seems to me that many White males negotiate their lives
without devoting much attention to feelings of vulnerability. Of
course, we tend not to disclose feelings to one another even if we
have them, so it may be that vulnerability is common but hidden.
In contrast, women and people of color seem to confront their
vulnerability as a matter of routine existence, learning to cope
with their reality in order to survive. I don't intend to make even
the slightest suggestion that having to cope with vulnerability provides some kind of advantage to such persons. I am more plagued

by my own sense of vulnerability and my difficulty in accepting it as human.

Resistance, Fear, Entitlement
Linda Calvert

There are real obstacles to engaging actively in diversity work in classrooms and beyond. Some of the resistances are subtle, some not so; some are personal, others structural; some because of fear, others because of entitlement. As an educator asking tough questions, I've engendered strong resistance. I have found it important to view what I do from a larger perspective, to know that what I do represents a commitment to a greater good—a society where all individuals have the opportunity to be who they are and what they can be, a place where organizations make sense for all people.

Deep Fear, Deep Hope
David Boje

This story is dedicated to the Black Student Union, the Belles, and Sircum Corda. They answered the call for a tutoring program at Nickerson. Thanks to Brenda Foster, Lupe, Brennan, Dan, Richard, Jon— the first students to get this off the ground. Thanks to Herbert Medina, Judith White, and Vickie Graf, professors who tutored and met with local principals for program support. Thanks to Nora King because it was her idea and to Brenda Jackson and Lucillia Hooper, who kept the peace when the kids and I got out of hand.

On the day of the Los Angeles riots of 1993, I got a phone call from Janetta at Nickerson Gardens: "Dave, don't come here today. It is not safe for you."

Nickerson Gardens is 66.5 acres of public housing in Watts in South Central Los Angeles. Five thousand people, rejected by an economy of racism, are condemned there to live on streets with cruel names like Success Avenue.

Mothers, keep your sons and daughters indoors today. LAPD archers are circling the camp. "David, Dennis Jackson and Tony Taylor were drinking beer in our parking lot when they got shot. LAPD said they got in the middle of their crossfire with snipers. No one saw snipers."

"What is happening there?" I asked.

"It's OK. We demanded the LAPD stay out of the development. The mothers took over. We are trying to keep youths calm. We formed a rumor clinic, and we're distributing food to the homeless."

Earlier that semester, my teaching assistant Reuben, Brenda Foster of Sircum Corda, and I had gone before the Nickerson Gardens Community. We outlined the Loyola Marymount University (LMU) tutoring program. Teams of LMU students and professors would come to Nickerson Gardens each week to tutor grades K through 12. Then the community voted.

Why? The residents believe in resident initiative. They decide which universities, media, and politicians come to their community. Every politician you can name has come to Nickerson. They promise $20 million, $60 million, $80 million in programs, jobs, training, child care, and who knows what. After the camera crews pack up, the money never trickles down to the community.

Residents have seen the media come and nickname their children "Li'l Half Dead," "Li'l Duke," "Half-Breed." They know the media boost circulation by getting their stories a little crooked, a little more gangland. Do they report the community's peacekeeping efforts? Do they report how this public-housing, high-poverty, no-jobs community collects food for people who do not have homes, how the residents build pride in their neighborhood, in their children, in themselves? No.

The community voted yes. We got Collegiate Press to print a thousand fliers on the community's own paper for half price. I hid the cost in one of my college budgets. Brenda put cartoons on it. Lupe translated it into Spanish. The flier looked good, and on a Wednesday afternoon, the students took off throughout the housing development to distribute the thousand copies. They ran door to door, talking to kids, greeting adults. "Hi. We're from LMU. Have you heard about the tutoring program? Here's a flier. Sign your kid up. Come on down. We will make learning fun for you." Enthusiasm, energy, courage.

I ran into the Resident Management Corporation (RMC) building and got several mothers together. "Please take care of the students. They are very naive about things." When I told them what the students had done, the mothers bolted out the door. Each took an LMU tutor by the hand and escorted him or her around their community. "These are Loyola Marymount students. They are here to work with the kids, for their tutoring." The students did not need LAPD officers to protect them. They were under the cover of the Mothers of the Hood.

Then came the riots. Brenda and Lupe asked me, "Are we going to tutor at Nickerson today?" "I don't know," I said. "Yesterday the LMU students got riot-flu. There is a lot of fear around LMU. Maybe we should cancel." Brenda and Lupe responded, "What kind of message would it send from LMU to Nickerson kids? We're too scared to come to tutor you today? We say go!" And we went.

The sun was shining. Mothers walked their kids home from school to the offices of the RMC and sat the kids at the tutoring tables. Jose, Edward, and other African-American and Latino children, twenty in all, crowded around a couple of tables with four LMU students. Books open, pencils all around.

This week, I noticed that Jose had cartoons he had drawn— Sagat, Ryu, Honda, a girl named Chun Li, and an Eskimo named Ken. I had an idea. Instead of candy, which always made the kids hyper and brought Ms. Hooper in to control the madness, I would distribute copies of Jose's 'toons. Jose and I went next door and began making copies. I made ten of Honda and asked Edward to go next door and distribute them. Pretty soon, Steve and Mike came in to complain, "Edward kept all the 'toons for himself. We didn't get any." "Edward," I said, "it is good to share!"

"Can I have twenty copies of Sagat?" "Me too!" "Me too!" A dozen boys were around me, screaming, "I want Honda." "I want twenty of Ryu." I asked, "How about four? I will make you each four. What will you do with the copies?" "Oh, we will give them to our friends at school. They can color them. Can I have ten more?"

I have been trying for weeks to work with Edward. He is old enough for second grade but still in first. He can write his name now, but when the mothers at the RMC began to tutor him, he could not copy an *A, B,* or *C.* I took Edward upstairs and got him going on the computer. He likes to run the mouse across my desk at high speed. He pounds it. I say, "Take it easy. Chill. The mouse is a delicate animal. Push it too hard and it won't breathe right." I reached out, took his hand in mine, and gently guided the mouse to pick up the ace of hearts off the video deck. Together we moved it to the place reserved for the first ace. "Now we can take that black king and put it in that space. This red queen you move on top of the king. After that, it's black, red, black, red, black, red." I let go of his hand. He seemed to get it.

Now I do not know if Microsoft Windows and Solitaire will improve Edward's reading. But if Edward keeps coming back and the LMU students keep crossing between our ivory tower and the Watts Tower, then there is hope.

Pain and Anger

*P*ain and anger are emotions we often don't like to talk about. We prefer to pretend they don't exist. In a socially constructed world—a world in which injustice and discrimination are common—pain and anger are inevitable. We experience pain personally. We feel pain for others. Pain is a source of anger. Anger is a signal for needed change.

Widespread taboos against expressing anger leave many of us with little experience in turning deep anger into developmental growth and learning. Instead, we have too many models for unproductive expressions of it. We lash out in ways that cause pain for others—pain to those who may deserve our anger or who innocently walk in the line of our fire. We deny or ignore anger, pulling inward and withdrawing into deadening depression. Pain, anger, pain, anger—the cycle easily continues. It can only be broken when pain is deeply felt and anger used for self-clarity and action.

Pain and anger are strange companions on the diversity teaching journey. As the contributors in this section suggest, pain and anger easily motivate and fuel passion. They can just as easily frighten and hinder good learning. Effective diversity educators feel pain and anger. They work through and with these emotions in their work, offering others models for authenticity and action.

Pain Motivates
David Boje

When my parents divorced and my mother, with four kids, slipped from rich surroundings in Paris to welfare and the land of White trash in Washington State, the new social context wrote a self into my being. My welfare voice outshouted my two years of culture in Paris and my easy childhood in Washington and Alaska. The level of surveillance into the personal self during welfare was invasive to the core of my being. When I was a teenager, a sloppy, White, mean, nasty welfare worker came into my house.

"Where is your room?" she asked as she headed for the bedrooms before I had a chance to answer. "Have you considered going to work to help out your mother? Anything you earn gets deducted from her check, but it's the right thing to do."

"I'm still in junior high," I replied. "I had a greenhouse job last summer." She was going through my bureau. She was touching my personal stuff. "Why are you doing this? That is my stuff!"

"It is just my job." She pulled out a transistor radio. "How much did this cost? It looks brand new."

"Thirteen dollars. I got it for my birthday." My body was shaking. My fists were clenched. I searched for words. My head was a hurricane. She read my temper and pulled away.

"This is just my job. I do what the county tells me to do. Don't blame me if you are breaking the rules. I have to report anything that is a diversion of AFDC funds into personal property. Radios are personal property. The amount will have to be deducted from your mother's check."

By the time I was seventeen, I had left home. Welfare does this. It divides families. Over the years, my rage seeped out when a motorist cut me off or someone looked at me weirdly. I had a chip on my shoulder from grade school well into adult life. Years of therapy and meditation helped. Getting back to the community and taking on the welfare and public housing bureaucracies settled my troubled spirit.

Discrimination Is Painful
Myrtle Bell

Ellis Cose's book *The Rage of a Privileged Class* (1993) touches my soul. Having read an excerpt, I purchased the book. Knowing that it would be painful, I did not open it for three months. Once I did, I could read only short parts at a time. It hurt too much. My generation thought education, hard work, and determination would even the playing field. To find that it has not brings rage. But rage is counterproductive unless focused and determined.

Then, too, there are negative aspects of having experienced the pain of discrimination that one tries to teach about. It is emotional and depressing. At times, I have to put my work and studies away. I have to focus on something with less personal meaning. Yet in life, there is no possibility of putting my race and sex away, waiting to deal with them at a more appropriate, less painful time.

The Work Is Painful for All
Earl Avery

Diversity teaching is painful for me personally at times. It's painful for the students that I'm teaching. As a responsible faculty member, I have to pay attention to the pain students endure. When we're planning a class, for example, we're very conscious of how many students of color are in the dialogue group. And if we're going do an exercise, we ask: What impact will it have on White students? What impact will it have on women? What impact will it have on students of color? All this takes its toll.

Part of the toll is the emotional stress that comes with wanting to open up a dialogue with our students in class. We've got to be willing to take risks, just as we're asking the students to take risks. We walk a fine line in terms of knowing how far we want to go or can go and still be able to maintain viable lines of communication with the class. That wears on you.

My identity is always an issue in each class. It has to be. Students say to us, "I want to hear your comments on such and such." They want to know our views because of our race or gender or both. Having your identity turned upside down, questioned, and looked at fifty different ways is not something that most faculty deal with.

Passion for the Work Is Fueled
Cliff Cheng

My anger and pain over being cast as the "other" are part of my passion for diversity work. The paradox is that anger both starts and blocks the healing power of love. Anger must be felt to be processed out. Unless I get angry, I cannot heal. If I get angry, I become even more marginalized.

I am frequently criticized for being too serious, too heavy, too intellectual. I cannot, however, take off my racial suit. I have to be on constant guard, checking to see if I am physically and emotionally safe, for there is no home in the "First World" or safe homeland in the "Third World" to go back to. The only measure of safety is *being* in the moment in the Tao.

A Help or a Hindrance in the Classroom?
Marcy Crary

I've said to Earl, the Black male member of our teaching team, that our students need to see and experience his anger. The three other members of our teaching team can help create a context for it and keep people safe while he expresses it.

I see myself, however, get silent around some male-female issues. If you were to ask about my silence, I'd say, "I don't know where I am. I'm not in touch with my feelings. I won't let myself get in touch with them." I know at other times I could be very angry, but I don't want to come across as such.

There's a part of me that wants to keep it all together, be cool and distant, work on creating the space to make other people comfortable. Draw them out. At the same time, I feel that by keeping it cool, we're losing a learning opportunity. Yet there's a risk. Anger is a risky emotion.

For some, however, maybe they'd really understand the issues if they heard the anger. We need to be able to talk openly about the anger, get our students to look at the very issue we're struggling with, join us on it. We would then teach them about the dilemmas and struggles we face—model the exact phenomena we're trying to explore.

Reflection as Necessity

Reflection is necessity for the diversity educator. It is no detour from essential work. It is a required way station along the route to self-awareness, authenticity, and good teaching. Reflection offers moments to stand back from the emotional demands of the work, consolidate new awareness, and struggle with old issues. It unearths deep, taken-for-granted assumptions. It replenishes the spirit, keeps the soul healthy, and feeds the mind. It is doing what we ask others to do in order to learn about workplace diversity. As the stories that follow remind us, reflection is a fact of life for diversity educators. It is a springboard to health, learning, and action.

Asking "Who Am I?" Rather Than "How Did I Do?"
Peter Couch

At the end of a recent summer session, I found myself thinking about the four African-American women who had been in a class of about thirty students. Four was an unusually high number: one or two is typical for our school. I mentally noted how well all four had done and even mentioned this to a friend. Later I felt embarrassed at having singled out the women for special recognition. Should I have been surprised? Did any other category of student perform just as well? Why do I even think of "categories" of students?

Suddenly another question occurred to me. Was my appraisal of the four women honest, or was I influenced by their skin color?

I now think that was in fact the case. Two of the four were top students, but the other two were average. I recognized that my support for the social "underdog" probably caused me to overreact toward minority students. Upon reflection, the need to keep a more balanced perspective became clear to me.

Is reflection critical to diversity work? Absolutely yes. I know I'm a reflective person. On Kolb's experiential learning model (1984), I score in the extreme as an observer-reflector. I tend to learn by looking and thinking about things. Reflection is an integral part of my learning process. My diversity learning typically builds on personal experience.

For me, several things contribute to being reflective about diversity. For one thing, my interests in understanding multiculturalism and diversity have increased significantly. The issues are important, and I am conscious of them almost all the time, it seems. Second, most of my "diversity experiences" (talking with students, trying a class exercise, discussing with a colleague, working with minorities, and so on) have emotional features. I "feel for" the problems and struggles of others. In fact, the emotional tone of these experiences triggers mental analysis. It encourages me to make sense and understand. Third, my efforts to reflect about diversity issues are strengthened by the possibility for actions to follow. I am motivated to think that I can do something as a result of my analysis.

Does diversity work take more self-reflection than other kinds of teaching? Yes. Diversity deals with our understanding of and our relationships with one another. There is high personal involvement in the work. I find it difficult to be objective or clinical when thinking about a diversity problem. I know that my values color my perceptions. Because of that, I know I need to think a great deal about how I see things. In contrast, if I want to help students learn something about the concept of systems thinking or the planning process, I'm less involved personally. My values still play a part in how I approach the subject, but the emotions involved are different. I may think about how I've handled the basic management issues in class, but my reflection about diversity teaching is much more likely to include reflection about myself—who I am—not just how I did.

Connecting Reflection to Action
Gordon Meyer

I'm uncomfortable with what feels like narcissism in my diversity work. Does being sensitive and embracing differences inevitably require a lot of self-exploration? Does "doing your own work" result in a self-reflective style that could be construed as, or eventually become, extreme self-centeredness? Are my concerns about self-absorption an outgrowth of the self-reflection necessary to write my contributions for this volume? Or are my concerns reflective of a more fundamental balancing act in learning about diversity?

I am coming to view critical self-reflection as essential to, but potentially distracting from, learning about and living with diversity. I am a teacher-scholar because I value the contemplative nature of the learning process. Such processes demand an openness to information about one's surroundings and actions and a willingness to reflect on that information. They also beg for openness to change. The requirements of learning and the norms of academia, however, can also provide a rationalization for "analysis paralysis." They can interfere with action, the source of further information. Self-reflection in the absence of experimenting with new behaviors is unlikely to lead to significant learning about how one can more effectively value those who are different.

Avoiding self-absorption and narcissism requires a vigilance toward action. It demands testing one's assumptions in the social world, something not entirely consistent with the culture of academia or many of our classrooms.

Understanding Our Own Identities
Lynda Moore and Bonnie Betters-Reed

Early in our work together, it became clear that we had to earn our stripes with women of color who also do the kind of work we do and with Afro-American women in general. As two White women, we have been confronted with anger by women of color who have challenged our authority and legitimacy to teach, research, and consult on the topic of multiculturalism among women. The harsh reality is that two White women working together could easily hide behind each other and remain distant and removed. In our enthusiasm and naïveté about our mission, we too often modeled a patronizing entitlement about diversity education. We also tended to underestimate the power and potential intimidation of our team.

Some colleagues of color made it clear they were not responsible for our enlightenment. As one Afro-American consultant, part of a focus group we were conducting, said, "You expect me to bleed for you, yet you have not even scratched the surface of your own lives." That was a turning point for both of us as we realized that we had not shared the pain and growth of our separate social and gender identities. And this was in part due to the fact that we had not done this work prior to asking others to do it for us.

Accepting Self-Reflection as a Fact of Life
Colleen Jones

I am exasperated being cast in a never-ending story as "Every Black Person." I have to overcome this feeling when I think about teaching diversity. That's probably why teaching a diversity course is something that I have not clamored to do. For me, there's too much of "me and mine" to become the "objective professor." My passion cannot be subdued.

Even though my courses are diversity-neutral by title ("Communications," "Organizational Behavior," "Leadership"), I now realize that regardless of what I teach, my students learn about diversity as a consequence of my presence in the classroom. That can be difficult to manage. I am who I am. Recognizing that students draw conclusions from my behavior keeps me in a constant state of reflection and introspection. Like a duck gliding across the water, I may seem cool, organized, and self-assured on the surface. Check below and I'm paddlin' like hell to stay afloat—trying to ensure that the images are affirmative, the messages are clear, the contexts are relevant, and the content is significant.

Seeing Self-Reflection as a Way of Life
Cliff Cheng

I reflect constantly. It is my nature to be contemplative. Meditative practice and writing are what I organize my life around, rather than the other way around. I find these cultural characteristics of contemplation to be at odds with the pace in the "First World." This is the only way, however, I can keep my sanity in the modernistic world.

Part V

Choosing the Work as the Journey

Sustaining Commitment

*D*iversity educators get tired and discouraged. Despite deep commitment, the pedagogical challenges, emotional intensity, and personal nature of the work take their toll. Learning is hard to measure, and progress is difficult to gauge. Activities that bring success one day seem like disasters the next. Students who defensively struggle to retain the comfort of old worldviews strike out angrily at instructors. Educators work hard to stay at least one step ahead of their students, juggling demands of personal learning with realities of classroom management. And although most educational and corporate settings are not hostile environments in which to do diversity teaching, few are fully supportive. Teaching workplace diversity is draining.

It is no surprise that effective diversity educators need ways of sustaining their commitment to the work. There are many possible sources of essential support and encouragement—team teaching, collaboration with trusted colleagues, developing precious allies, reframing the way we view the work, integrating multiple parts of our lives, changing work venues, keeping harsh realities ever present, practicing meditation.

A primary means for sustaining commitment is connections with others who do like-minded work. Friendships and support networks keep us balanced and on track, with the added benefit of sustaining fellow travelers along the way.

Precious Allies
Barbara Walker

Diversity work can lead to burnout. One of the most important ways of avoiding burnout is to stay connected with people I regard as *precious allies*. These are my colleagues who share the vision, give me straightforward and honest feedback, help me strategize, support and nurture me, and celebrate with me all our little accomplishments!

Words that Maya Angelou once spoke to me also sustain me. Years ago, I met her at the invitation of my sister-in-law, who was a student in one of her classes. Maya seemed to be especially interested in the work I was doing, and our discussion led us to the subject of creativity. When I told her how much I enjoyed her poetry and admired her creativity, she shot back: "Oh, no, I'm not creative. My brother is the creative one. I'm able to sort through what everyone else says and just put it back together differently." She was so straightforward and clear about her gift that her words still ring in my ears. Her different approach to creativity helped me think differently about my own contributions.

Friendship, Support, and Feminist Interdependence
Bonnie Betters-Reed and Lynda Moore

Sometimes the two of us do not sustain each other's commitment to diversity education—we just plain sustain the commitment to our friendship and keep each other going. We have a pattern of living our work, which means that we do not separate our numerous agendas. During our nine years together, we have always kept at least one joint diversity project going. We have met, or at least had one telephone meeting, every week. We begin every meeting with personal sharing of critical incidents or pressing deadlines. We listen to each other, and when we feel ready, we put our nose to the grindstone and wrap up another project. We know we'll feel better and more able to cope with our daily stress.

Increasing our self-awareness and understanding of each other has helped us integrate our diversity journey with our lives. For both of us, the deeper levels of self-disclosure and trust that have emerged as a result of practicing what we preach in the classroom enable us to see diversity issues in all phases of our lives. Similar to our feminist approach of working together, we provide support and companionship for each other's parenting journey. We can critically discuss our family lives, saying things about each other's kids, spouses, and interactions that we would not accept from others. For example, our eight-year-old sons are very different. Their lack of common interests and contrasting social styles frequently resulted in conflict when we were all together. We were able to talk about it and make suggestions rather than allow their differences to separate us as families.

The differences and similarities we encounter in our own lives help us in our classrooms as well. We model for our students the challenge of valuing other people, friends included, and the work it takes to sustain meaningful relationships.

Working together as a team at the same institution enables us to take turns renewing and expanding our interests in diversity education. For Lynda, the repetition of her required undergraduate course on managing the pluralistic workforce has been augmented by new readings and insights from our joint work. And when Bonnie could not teach a graduate course on multiculturalism due to administrative responsibilities, she recommended that Lynda do so. In turn, next semester, Bonnie will prep a new international management course that is highly influenced by Lynda's experience with her intercultural seminar. Both of us clearly benefit from one of us preparing a new diversity-related course.

Increasingly, we are becoming bolder with our classroom experimentation as a result of enacting feminist interdependence in our lives and work. We recently decided to focus on diversity among women entrepreneurs. The newness and timeliness offered revitalization, challenge, and a new synergy for our expertise and background.

No Choice: High Stakes for All
Myrtle Bell

Sustaining personal commitment after a lifetime of pain and fighting is tiring. Lacking alternatives and having children, I choose to continue the fight. For fleeting moments, I think it would be easier to hide, no longer to educate people about the rights and feelings of others, about the consequences of discrimination. I know, however, that for the sake of the children, I must continue. I also realize that to teach well, perhaps best, one must feel the issues. Having experienced firsthand the pain of discrimination, I can explain it.

Sustaining personal commitment is hard when so many people in power believe that discrimination no longer exists in American workplaces. These people seem unaware of the reality of discrimination: the cents on the dollar and the returns on education that women and persons of color earn compared with White men. What they focus on is perceptions of "reverse discrimination" or the myth of Black women being "doubly advantaged"—receiving affirmative action credit for both their race and gender. Sustaining personal commitment is hard in light of all this.

At the same time, however, I see my commitment bolstered by being Black and female, doubly disadvantaged, subject to both racial and sexual discrimination. If I, a Black woman who may be more personally affected than other groups, am too tired to continue to try, who will?

People today seem to have a prejudice against prejudice. Most, particularly white-collar professionals, really believe that people who practice discrimination do not last in organizations. We do not want to acknowledge that within us, there may be complicity or even active participation in discrimination. We prefer to believe that people's lack of progress is due to internal factors and a lack of skills, such as saying "ax" instead of "ask." Yet persistent disparities in earnings, the reality that higher-paying male jobs become lower-paying jobs when women assume them, and the large number of women and minorities who populate lower organizational levels are evidence to me that something, whatever we may choose to call it, other than fairness regularly occurs in many, if not most, organizations.

What helps me sustain my commitment most is a fear deep inside me that despite the increasing heterogeneity of the workforce, nothing may change at the top. It would be horrific, but not impossible, for the year 2050 to arrive with the ratios of White males in positions of power to all other people similar to what we find today.

Meditation to Start Each Day Anew
Cliff Cheng

I need a strong meditative practice to counter the despair of the pain of "otherness." Meditative practice is at the center of my life and creativity. Rather than organize my life around the rat race of trying to eat higher on the food chain, I find sanity within. Clarity comes from sitting in meditation. The emotions and projections of the day dissipate so I can rest peacefully at night. Awakening fresh to the new day, without the residue of the previous day's unresolved emotions and thoughts, enables the Tao, the creative process, to start each day anew.

Collaboration and Community Building

*C*ollaboration is a rich source of insight. It is also the main ingredient for creating and sustaining a community of learning necessary to support diversity education. It is not always easy to achieve, however, in a society that champions individual achievements and initiative. Indices of professional success and reward systems in both academic and corporate arenas, for example, too often underestimate the creative synergy from true collaboration. It is sometimes defined in disparaging terms— the weaker player gets a free ride. A search may be mounted to identify and reward the "real force" behind the outcome. The implicit message is clear: success requires "going it alone."

Features in the diversity teaching and learning process and the evolving nature of the field itself contribute their own potential impediments to collaboration. The intense and personal nature of the work can keep educators focused inward—too exhausted or too vulnerable to reach out. Differences in definition, focus, and approach to the work make it easy to overlook possible opportunities and reasons for collaboration. Pioneers, who have worked alone and developed individual styles and coping strategies by necessity, may find it hard to break those patterns. Newcomers to the field may not know where to go.

There are many ways to develop and strengthen connections to those who share passions and commitments to diversity teaching. Service and consulting activities, team teaching, and collaborative writing projects bring diversity educators together to exchange ideas, stories, and learning.

Exchanging readings, resources, and syllabi enables educators to learn from one another. Conferences and professional associations provide space for kindred spirits to gather and reconnect. Phone calls or face-to-face conversations serve some. For others, e-mail offers an ongoing way to share experiences, test ideas, and solicit feedback.

The key is for diversity educators not to see themselves as alone but to identify ways to connect with like-minded colleagues. We all have opportunities to develop and facilitate these connections. The contributors in this section are clear about the benefits of doing so.

Across Our Differences
Marcy Crary

We were in a discussion group together. It hit me profoundly how much I needed Earl because—and I think I said this at the time—of the inadequacy of my own White woman's view of reality. And that's true of everybody. We all need each other across our differences. It is difficult to see what we have not experienced because of our skin color, ethnicity, or other difference. I appreciate over and over what we've created for ourselves by starting the course and how it has played out in terms of our relationships over time.

Creative Synergy
Lynda Moore

Our personal and professional relationship has grown and deepened over our nine years together. We have come to recognize our similarities and differences and have learned to work together creatively and synergistically with both.

We both share a passion for making a contribution to women's lives and their advancement. We also share a deep and abiding interest in culture in all its varied forms. We express this through our teaching, research, administration, and consulting as well as in activities with our families. We have also shared our mutual struggle for balance in our lives as working mothers and continue to question the meaning and role of work in our lives. As we take time to enjoy our children more, we become better at setting priorities at work and sticking to them. We also share a need for change in our lives: we need to find new and challenging activities that excite us.

Our differences stem largely from cultural background and personal style. My dress is more formal and more conservative than Bonnie's. My orientation is more individualistic; Bonnie's, collaborative. I worked alone prior to collaborating with Bonnie and found the transition more difficult than I imagined. It was particularly evident in my language as I continued to say "I" rather than "we" when discussing joint work. Although it was embarrassing to be confronted about my noncollaborative language, it was an important step in developing our relationship.

As chair of the Management Department, Bonnie's managerial style was task-oriented and tough. Yet in her interpersonal relationships and her teaching, Bonnie is very demonstrative and warm. In contrast, my communication style is more formal and impersonal in teaching contexts. I am similar to Bonnie in my interpersonal relationships. We have enjoyed learning about our similarities and differences. We have learned to value and benefit from each other's feedback and skills. We recognize that we still model the image of a more aloof and personally detached "professional" in some of our roles. We are learning to let go of White male metaphors for professional behavior and to model the value of living our own cultural identity for ourselves and others.

Community
Cliff Cheng

As I support your travels as your journey person and you do the same for me, we recognize that we are here to play parts in the drama and comedy of one another's lives. True diversity comes from the heart, from supporting one another in the formation, sustenance, and renewal of community that is based on interdependence, intimacy, and communion, not on instrumental, economic, or psychological needs. We truly value differences only when this is done.

Joys and Benefits of the Work

*A*s the stories of the contributors so powerfully convey, there is great *joy in diversity teaching. The satisfaction and enjoyment of working at the interface of personal development and social change can more than balance the intensity and challenges of the work.*

The joys are varied. They are easy to forget as we focus on individual exchanges, students, classes, and learning moments. They are easier to see when we stand back, take a long-term perspective on our own and students' learning, and explore the implications of all that we have done. Lives have changed. Eyes have opened. Connections have multiplied. Possibilities for a better world are expanded. Our own lives have become more authentic, connected, deep, vibrant.

The road is not easy. The journey is long. Ah, but the benefits of travel are sweet.

Sharing in Others' Self-Discovery and Growth
Dina Comnenou

My greatest joy is the learning and growth of my students and clients. They become captured by self-discovery and human diversity. One example of a joyful instance took place in a weeklong corporate "human interaction workshop." The twelve participants varied in age, culture, race, sex, and socioeconomic background.

191

A young White male in the session struggled with his reluctance to share deep feelings and thoughts in the group. As days went on, his own curiosity, as well as his trust in the group's integrity and support, grew stronger. He gradually let go of his reticence and became quite committed to his own learning, as well as that of the group.

When a somewhat older, more experienced African-American woman encountered similar reluctance in herself, several group members tried to help. The young White male was the only one who could effectively reach her. He literally held her in the safety of his own experience and triumph over fear. Seemingly separated by race, gender, age, and life trajectory, they put their arms around each other and marveled in the pleasure of sharing their reticence in the group as well as deeply personal and painful childhood traumas. Tears streamed down their cheeks; then smiles erupted. Their parallel experiences gave them a unique understanding of each other. The divisions of age, race, gender, and background became enriching differences for them. They helped these two individuals understand new facets of their problems and experiences. They were surprised, moved, and, above all, connected. As the life and work of the group progressed, they confronted and explored the differences between them. They sat together, however, and often kept their arms around each other. Change was noticeable in both of them. Their faces had mellowed. Their bodies had loosened. Their voices were warmer.

As I looked at the transformation, I remembered the suspicion they both had about each other in the beginning of the lab. They had both noted deep divisions of race, life experience, language, and style in the group. They still had a long way to go, but they had started wrestling with these differences and had come out learning what only they could teach one another. I felt greatly rewarded, lucky to have shared in this joy, and proud to have, in some small way, contributed to their learning as they had to mine.

Making a Difference
Myrtle Bell

It is extremely rewarding to know that I've made a difference in someone's life and thinking. I believe that for every one person who is enlightened, a myriad of people will benefit. Knowledge cascades and multiplies. Helping people understand the need to "value" diversity is very rewarding.

My greatest joy in diversity teaching is having learned some things for myself. It was a relief to read research that discusses why race and ethnic relations appear to be worse now. We may see relations as worse because we expect them to be so much better. It is a relief to read and analyze patriarchal- and capitalist-based theories of gender domination. Learning about rational bias helps me understand, but not agree with, those who claim reverse discrimination. Trying to make sense of the senseless and unresolvable is soothing.

Learning, for Me and Others
Peter Couch

There are times when students demonstrate surprise and interest in something they hadn't thought much about. They show signs of growing awareness of difficulties faced by others. They demonstrate their desire to learn about and deal with racial problems. Minority students seem pleased to have a chance to express their perceptions candidly. Picking up such cues from students is rewarding. On a personal level, there is the joy of discovery, of gaining new insights, of moving up a level or so in terms of understanding. There is the joy of learning—from colleagues and from an intriguing and thoughtful article or book.

Making a Difference in the Worlds We Create
Marcy Crary

Students leave our course being in very different places. Some are impassioned missionaries and some are conflicted discontents, but all see the world a little differently. I get a great sense of satisfaction when I hear students really grappling actively in the classroom with their own emotional responses to diversity issues and when they talk about their taking action to make a change in some relationship, group, or work setting where they witness basic injustice.

I love participating in active reflection and dialogue about our everyday practices and constructions of reality, particularly when I feel that the result of such work may make a difference in the quality of the worlds we create together. Diversity work at its best is work that expands one's heart, mind, and quality of action.

Watching One Student Take a Giant Step
Earl Avery

I won't say joy, but I think what makes me feel good about doing the work is when I have the opportunity, at the end of the semester, to look closely at one or two students who have really taken giant steps in terms of their development. I get a certain satisfaction from that. There's also satisfaction in knowing that we as a team have had a good semester.

Discovering the Joy of My Chineseness
Cliff Cheng

I desire the healing power of feeling and expressing the joy of my Chineseness. I am in the process of discovering what this means. This is why I am on the diversity learning and teaching journey. No one can teach me this, for those around me have to some degree had their minds colonized by communism, capitalism, and Western religion and culture. I must find this joy myself in the Way.

Feeling Fully Alive
Gordon Meyer

There are many joys for me. One is the joy of feeling fully alive and present. I have an insatiable appetite for knowing that I am a feeling, capable, and caring person. I find diversity work gratifying and growthful when my openness and willingness to work on issues of accepting and valuing others who are different seem to catalyze new relationships. I also get great satisfaction from situations in which my doing my diversity work seems to open up the possibility of others' doing their own work. When students, for example, suggest that my being more open in the classroom has invited them to see another person in a new way or confront a situation that they might otherwise have avoided, I feel real pride and satisfaction.

Finding Integration and Authenticity
Lynda Moore and Bonnie Betters-Reed

The personal joy we receive from teaching about diversity is seeing the growth and development of our students. Because we are at a women's college, our mission is aligned with our institutional mission. Our work is seen not only as a strength in our program but as a contribution to the college as well.

A rich outcome of our diversity work has been the individual journey each of us has taken, searching for integration of our diversity values with all aspects of our lives. As we began to experience the feelings of true feminist identity and collaboration, we tried to live this in our daily lives with our children, spouses, friends, family, and colleagues. We are both at midlife, when the question "what's next?" or "so what?" is ever present. Engaging in diversity teaching and writing has provided a reason to embrace these questions and celebrate our journey toward greater integration and authenticity. Doing diversity work means doing our own work around our racial, ethnic, gender, and cultural identities. It means becoming truer to ourselves. For Lynda, this has manifested in greater experimentation in her career. For Bonnie, this has meant coming to terms with the freedom and ability to see her "nondiversity" courses through a diversity lens, to teach strategy or leadership as a feminist. It has also meant finding peace with herself through activities she really wanted to do, such as increased spiritual work and community involvement.

Looking at the Faces, Listening to the Stories
David Boje

Joy: seeing the faces of the seven public housing residents who completed our workshops and got those jobs in the Housing Authority, hearing my students tell their stories about work on the "Babies and Mothers with AIDS" class project, getting a hug from Nora, talking to C. Z. Wilson about my career and family choices, seeing residents of public housing stand up and become workshop facilitators, watching the Peace Corps Fellows work with the residents, playing with the kids when the Loyola Marymount student tutors try to work with them on their homework.

Enjoying the Company
Linda Calvert

I would like to say that I have made a big difference. That hasn't happened. I have, however, experienced crystalline moments when personal truth came home, small groups suddenly "got it," exercises caused people to think in new ways, and students opened up to me because I understood or could be trusted—catching me in the hall, following me to my office, telling me what they have discovered, asking questions, coming back for more. Student journals are treasure troves filled with new perspectives about everyday life, warm and connective humor, and the richest and deepest of human thoughts, memories, feelings, and insights. I watch students in experiential exercises or in group processing sessions when the *aha!* of an experiential moment suddenly registers or the words of a fellow student hit home. These are moments of pure gold.

The rest of the joy has little to do with what I have accomplished. I continue to learn things that astonish and heal me. And one of the greatest joys is my friends. When I look around or call someone on the phone, I see and hear people I can trust. They are people who hear me, support me, are honest with me, or just laugh with me. I learn from these people. I know myself in new ways. I like the company.

Creating a Richer, More Interesting World
Duncan Spelman

Principally, the joys are the people. Being involved in diversity work has connected me to a circle of people that is richer, more interesting, and more alive than the world in which I lived before. And these people carry a vision of civilization that seems to me to be the only true hope for humanity—a worldview based on community and interdependence rather than on individualism and independence. Having this vision as an active component in my life rescues me from the despair resulting from the many ways in which we do not live together.

Discovering the Self, the Soul
Barbara Walker

Learning to love people because of their differences, and sometimes in spite of their differences, is hard work, but it rewards us well along the way. The personal joy for me in this work is the journey itself. Joy comes in the discovery of the self—the soul—along the way.

I feel great joy that I was in the right place at the right time and thus had the privilege to play a key role as a leader in the unfolding of this work. But the greatest joy of all has been the extraordinary friendships developed in the process of doing this work—authentic, significant, interdependent relationships that grew because of the differences among us. Many of these friendships are still in place. By far, one of the most important of these is the relationship that developed among four women—two White and two Black—all managers at Digital Equipment Corporation. Our story is a powerful one. It began with the almost stereotypical enmity between us as White and Black women. Today we are spiritual sisters.

Knowing That Some Part of Me Stays with You
Colleen Jones

At times, my intuition tells me that a student, a colleague, or an associate is undergoing an intellectual awakening with respect to difference and diversity because of me. That is extremely gratifying, even though the transformation toward being more accepting of diversity may be ephemeral without environmental reinforcement or more work for a "complete conversion." My greatest joy, however, comes from knowing that some part of me—something I said, did, or suggested as a reading to a student—will always be with that person and maybe, just maybe, will make her or him think positively about differences or act affirmatively to promote diversity.

Being All of Me with All of Thee
Darlyne Bailey

Joy is the permission, freedom, right, and responsibility to be all of me with all of thee. What more can anyone ask for?

Future Directions

We began this project with a journey metaphor, convinced from our own work and experiences that teaching and learning about workplace diversity involve an ongoing voyage of discovery and change. The story of the journey is one of never arriving. Challenges mark the travel. Old maps no longer guide us. We negotiate critical crossroads and choice points; what we choose affects where we go. We sustain ourselves on the road; it is easy to lose faith on the long uphill climbs. As we go, we savor new and assorted views, enjoy the companionship of fellow travelers, take comfort when we can in our progress, and relish the unexpected along the way.

The contributors to this book confirmed our experiences. They, too, saw their diversity work as a journey—a journey of personal and professional learning and growth, for themselves, for their students and clients, and for the discipline as a whole. Their energy and joy lay in the traveling.

The final set of stories explore the contributors' perspectives on the future of their diversity teaching journeys. Taken as a whole, they provide a powerful vision for the future of diversity education.

The stories vary as the storytellers do. Some report specific agendas for their own diversity work. Some relay thoughts about the future of the discipline itself. Others speak of future plans in more personal terms. All the stories, however, have one consistent theme: each describes diversity education as an integral and ineradicable part of the teller's life. Just as *the contributors' present journeys are rich and diverse, so will be their futures and ours.*

Keep a Door Open to New Ideas
Earl Avery

I don't know what diversity work is going to be like in ten or twenty years. I don't even know what it's going be called. Certainly the issue of aging is one area where my thinking will likely expand. Age differences in our society become more of an issue all the time. As to race, I see myself continuing to learn through exploration, trying different behaviors, reflecting on what I've been doing and how I've been doing it, and maintaining a certain level of openness that allows me to broaden my thinking.

As I get older, the real challenge is keeping the door open for new ideas. It's very easy to fall into thinking, "Well, I've been around, so now I know it all. I've seen it before." Staying out of that trap, keeping an open mind, and pushing my thinking will be the challenge for me. It's a challenge for us all.

Beyond that, I just haven't thought that far in the future or about what my destiny will be. It would be nice to go through a period of my life not always having to think about race, gender, and all the other differences. I know that's not reality. There is still a great deal that I can learn from others. That's what I'm going to do. Keep my mind open and learn from others.

Celebrate the Interconnectedness of Life
Darlyne Bailey

This journey seems to mirror my sense of who I am in relation to others. That leads to more information about why I am here on this planet, in this way, at this time. Where I hope to be heading is toward the ability to engage actively with others in the moment-to-moment celebration of the interconnectedness of life!

Continue the Journey
Myrtle Bell

My destination in diversity work is to educate as many people as I can through classroom teaching and through day-to-day living. The journey is continual. I am a student as well as an instrument of learning.

Bring Diversity into the Center
Bonnie Betters-Reed and Lynda Moore

Our goal is to continue the route of integration, to bring diversity education into the center of teaching and learning. We want students to learn to see the world through a multicultural lens, to understand the transferability and empowerment of the concepts of inclusion and valuing of differences. Our next project is to focus on diversity among women in the entrepreneurial field. Beyond this, we are not sure where we are headed. We know, however, that our partnership will transcend personal and professional choices. Our journey is so intertwined and our mutual understanding and support of each other are so key to our continued exploration that we will remain kindred souls in whatever the future holds.

Take Education into the Community
David Boje

Ivan Illich was right. We have to take university education out of ivory towers and into the community (Illich, 1971). We are quickly descending into a two-class society of haves and have-nots. When we could cut military spending and rebuild public schools, we cut senior citizen benefits to give tax breaks to the well-to-do. We build prisons instead of schools. I cannot stomach organizational behavior or theory any longer. I do not want to participate in training people to imitate the leaders of AT&T, IBM, and GM as they strategically downsize, "right-size," and reengineer things so that a few rich cats earn money off the twenty-five-cent-an-hour workers in China, Indonesia, and other Third World countries. All this while in our own United States we build a permanent underclass of underemployed and entrapped youth in our inner cities. The whole thing is a nightmare out of a Stephen King novel.

Where do I see myself heading? Back to public housing. This is the front line of the diversity action. I will continue to get my university more intertwined with the public housing community. My journey? I am an outsider. I do not fit in; nor do I want to. If I fit in, I fear I will lose my perspective.

Focus on Personal Growth and Social Commitment
Linda Calvert

My diversity work is about personal growth and social commitment. Since I see our society as deteriorating in many ways, I don't see myself or us "getting there" anytime soon. I could speak more eloquently about being on a lifelong journey; however, the truth is that I get tired watching the world take one step forward and two steps back. So I focus on different aspects of the journey—sometimes on me, sometimes on larger diversity issues, sometimes on other things.

In all this, I've noticed that I am less sure about where I am going or how to get there. I am not goal-directed in the rational fashion that I once thought important. I've also noticed that the "crowd" around me is smaller and looks different: there are fewer males and a broader mix of races and ethnicities. I feel comfortable.

I'm not sure where I am going, nor am I sure about the twists and turns of the path, but I like the company.

Make a Difference Within Myself
Cliff Cheng

My future work has not been revealed to me. I have not gotten there yet. It will likely not take me down the same White "male-stream" road that my present colleagues travel, but this is not my concern—not the concern of someone in the Tao, on the inner spiritual journey of learning and growth.

I've come to realize that the only difference I can make is within myself. I am not going to save the world or end racism and masculinity discrimination through my consulting, teaching, writing, marriage, or children. The only thing I can do is get clear in the moment and do no harm to others. If others deeply want to change their *being* and I can help them as their journey person, then I am available to be of service.

I do not see a final end to the diversity teaching and learning journey. All I see is the process of *being* in the Tao and therefore in my higher nature or existing outside the Tao in my lower, human nature. I don't believe in the myth of progress. It's a carrot at the end of the stick, a dog chasing its own tail. I'll always be on the journey in this lifetime. Human nature cannot be transcended, only incorporated and made part of the path.

Be Less Silent
Dina Comnenou

One of the frustrating by-products of having grown up in a Greek culture in which racial strife was not a central part of the context has been a different process of racial identity development than most of my colleagues from the United States. My society of origin was by no means less racist. Racial attitudes, however, were based on a belief system different from the one in which I presently work. As I use material and concepts developed in the United States, I find that they are useful in understanding the experiences of individuals whose racial identity developed in this country. They do not, however, necessarily apply to my own racial learning. Consequently, at times I feel that my own personal racial learning is stifled by the racial environment of the United States. I am asked to learn others' lessons, not mine.

I often find that I am the only person from my culture in the workplace and in other groups. Being in the minority is an enormous problem, as it prevents one's issues from being validated or reality-tested. I have been publicly silent about my racial learning and have explored my identity along these lines on my own. In my future development, I would like to be less silent about sharing those issues with others.

Understand More
Peter Couch

It seems reasonable to me to think of my diversity work as being on a journey. There's no specific target or end point. I simply want to know, to understand more about the human condition. I have a lot of curiosity. I won't be teaching for many more years. Teaching has been a major outlet, a chance to take action, to apply some of the things I've learned about diversity. I'll have to find other ways to use what I learn.

Be Comfortable with Being Uncomfortable
Marcy Crary

An issue most central to my concerns about doing diversity work is my own comfort level working with others on difference issues. I've taught this diversity course ten times now. I still have a fundamental anxiety about what I am up to in this work. I continue to feel "not good enough." I wish I could feel that I'm on more solid ground. This feeling is hard to explain or understand.

On the one hand, I feel a strong commitment to and passion about the importance of this kind of learning for all. On the other hand, I don't feel that I've found the way to do this teaching that fits me best. I don't feel that I'm teaching from my strengths. I'm not sure if this is because I'm a member of a team, it's a big class, or our design and scripts for the course don't fit the way I like to teach. I don't often feel successful up in front of the class. The short of it is that I struggle to make sense of this fundamental uncertainty I feel about my diversity teaching effectiveness. Maybe I'll never feel totally good enough. Maybe the people in the room are at such different levels of awareness that they need too many different things from us as teachers. Maybe I'm overly attuned to what's happening in the classroom and feel too responsible for it. Perhaps, however, I just need to learn to be comfortable being uncomfortable. Perhaps all these feelings go with the territory. The combination of teaching this course and teaching it with a diverse team creates a context of continuous learning.

Express What and Who I Am
Colleen Jones

My mother said it when I was in elementary school. I shuddered at the thought in college. I finally admitted it in my thirties. I live it now. I am a teacher! I have been since my student activist days, when I gestured with a clenched fist, "Knowledge Is Power!" "Black Is Beautiful!" "Power to the People!" The fact that I consider all of my teaching diversity teaching speaks volumes about how much this is an expression of what and who I am. Consequently, I hope to become a more masterful sailor on this rough sea of life. I want to continue picking up passengers willing to do more than merely come along for the ride. I want fellow travelers who will actively explore new, unfamiliar, or uncomfortable territories. As long as I can talk, I'll be doing that.

Be Fully Present
Gordon Meyer

My destination is to be more fully present and human in my encounters with others. I want to be open to others for myself. I want to grow as an individual. I want to create opportunities for others to feel fully accepted—spaces where they can grow because they feel valued for who they are and what they believe to be their unique potential.

Being fully present and human involves sharing vulnerability in feeling that I am different in ways that don't always feel safe. I recall a conversation I had with my mother when I was fifteen or sixteen years old. I wanted something different from relationships than many of my male friends: my male peers didn't want to share feelings or vulnerabilities with me or their other male friends. I yearned for such relationships. I felt different and uncomfortable because I was utterly convinced that my peers would reject me if they understood my desire for deep and caring companionship. I now understand intellectually that many men have felt (and continue to feel) as I did. I hope that my journey will take me to a place where I am comfortable sharing feelings and struggles toward greater self-knowledge in ways that make it possible for others to learn about themselves and others in deeper ways than they might have otherwise. At my present way station on this journey, I believe that I do my best diversity work when I connect with my past or present feelings of loneliness, pain, and vulnerability.

Face Each New Day
Duncan Spelman

The image that seems to fit best is of a journey without a destination. It's clearly a journey—something new each day, much to be learned, long distances to be traveled. It feels, however, like a trip through such complex terrain that no adequate map exists to guide the way. The territory is truly uncharted. The landscape seems always to be changing—not just because I'm moving but because the landscape itself is constantly reforming. The diversity course we teach feels uphill too. The travel is hard work. Ultimately, however, there is no choice about whether the journey is to be undertaken. This is not a vacation trip, chosen and controlled. It's what's waiting each morning as I open my eyes to a new day.

Learn to Deal with the Honorable Opposition
Barbara Walker

As we try to figure out where diversity work is heading, we must not forget that the work is the legacy—the child—of affirmative action in the workplace. Concerns about the numbers and representation of protected-class groups in the workplace have broadened into a philosophy of inclusion and synergy. Given the constancy of change, we know that diversity work, too, will change and evolve into another form.

For now it appears that diversity, as a broader and more inclusive approach to the work of dealing with differences in the workplace, continues to touch a central nerve in organizations and educational institutions across America. These organizations recognize the strategic benefits of diversity work.

Some of the more successful small companies in Silicon Valley, for example, acknowledge the importance of caring about employees and the role that diversity plays in creating a special organizational spirit. Leaders in these organizations recognize that a nurturing, caring environment is an essential ingredient for productivity. Today, as more and more people draw a sense of identity from their work, the yearning for connection is a critical workplace reality. When people feel valued, they bring the best of themselves to their work. When they have been accepted for who they are, when they feel heard and see that their issues have been taken seriously, then, and only then, are they open to real change. One of my favorite learning-to-value-differences stories is a real-life saga of "The Klansman and the Cantor." It tells of how a bitter, bigoted man changed his views simply because another man cared enough to build a meaningful relationship with him.

The world has become so complex that we must learn to balance our personal values with the ability to share the world peacefully. Just as diversity work helps us accept the reality of change, perhaps it can also help us accept the fact that some things never change. The realities of the nature of conflict and competition mean that there will always be some people who do not value others and insist on seeing them as enemies. Alan Watts, a contemporary philosopher, has noted that to love your enemies means just that—loving them as enemies. In his wonderful book titled *The Book* (1966), Watts advises us never to fail to honor the opposition or regard it as entirely evil or demented:

> Hatreds are not going to be healed, but only inflamed, by insulting those who feel them, and the abusive labels with which we plaster them—squares, fascists, rightists, know-nothings—may well become the proud badges and symbols around which they will rally and consolidate themselves. Nor will it do to confront the opposition in public with polite and non-violent sit-ins and demonstrations, while boosting our collective ego by insulting them in private. If we want justice for minorities and

cooled wars with our natural enemies, whether human or non-human, we must first come to terms with the minority and the enemy in ourselves and in our hearts, for the rascal is there as much as anywhere in the "external" world—especially when you realize that the world outside your skin is as much yourself as the world inside [p. 133].

We have so much more work to do in learning how to deal with the honorable opposition.

Final Thoughts

Listening to the Soul, Speaking from the Heart

Throughout this project, we have been continually surprised, delighted, and informed by important insights about the joys and complexities of teaching workplace diversity. Our work has been filled with respect for the contributors to this volume, growing awareness of all that we have yet to learn, and satisfaction in having taken on this challenge.

We end with reflections on what we have learned from all this. In this final section, we explore the importance of a strong pedagogy of learning, the foundation for and important contributions of diversity education, the need to become more multicultural, the central role of paradox, the importance of preparation and faculty development, the essential need for community, and the future of the work.

A Strong Pedagogy of Learning

We began this project to explore the teaching of workplace diversity. We end it knowing the impossibility of separating teaching and learning in diversity education. Teachers learn. Students teach. Traditional classroom distinctions blur. The complexity and unpredictability of the issues leave educators no choice but to learn while they work. Opportunities for personal and professional learning are never-ending. This ongoing learning is a distinctive feature of the work for many of us and one of its major fascinations.

Diversity education therefore demands a strong pedagogy of learning. It includes understanding how people learn. It involves helping others learn how to learn something as complex and deep as diversity, how to learn in different and multiple ways, and how to embrace continuous learning. Individuals bring different learning styles and starting points to the classroom. Successful diversity educators understand, respect, and work with those differences. They also model what they teach.

A strong pedagogy of learning needs to reflect that diversity learning occurs on many levels: personal and emotional, cognitive and conceptual, interpersonal and social, structural and institutional. Pace, process, timing, content, focus, and learning goals are all influenced by the ways in which individuals learn differently on each level.

Because learning about workplace diversity is not a linear process, the different kinds and levels of learning occur simultaneously. Teachers and learners move back and forth between explorations of deeply personal experience and the larger social and institutional implications. Effective diversity educators encourage people to feel and know, to think and act, to look inward and focus outward. They work for intrapersonal and interpersonal awareness. They push to examine the implications for institutional and social change. Such work demands pedagogical flexibility. Skills and techniques for responding to individual pain or fear, for example, are different from those for abstracting broad principles or generalizing from an intense, personal moment. Competencies required to learn about our own perceptions and biases are different from those needed to encourage others to do the same.

A strong pedagogy of learning also asks educators to be both conceptually and personally grounded in the diversity issues they teach. We have been continuously reminded in this project that diversity education is both complicated and emotionally charged. The challenge is to make the complex manageable but not simplistic—to offer safe entry into the complexity and a supportive platform from which to dive deeper into the issues. Sharing personal examples, developing metaphors, examining data, and exploring grounded models are ways to bring manageability to the process. So is open discussion about the ongoing nature of diversity learning for all.

The contributors remind us throughout this volume that their diversity learning came over time and at a price. Patience, empathy, respect for the winding road to knowledge, and willingness to share learning difficulties along the way serve diversity educators well in their teaching.

First Things First: Being, then Doing

The best learning journeys lead to new destinations. We began this project wanting to know what constituted good diversity teaching. We envisioned providing readers with a realistic sense of the work and hoped to influence what people do in their classrooms and training sessions. The contributors' stories, however, led us to a different path. They demanded that we focus more on *who the diversity educator is* than on what the educator does. This book ultimately says more about the importance of being than doing. Identity and personal grounding are the foundations for effective diversity education.

Diversity education, of course, involves *doing*. Good materials, techniques, skills, and well-crafted exercises are important in diversity teaching. We believe, however, that management educators have become too focused in recent years on techniques and activities. Diversity education demands something deeper.

Teaching workplace diversity requires a different mind-set and heart-set. Success does not come from requiring just the right book, adopting a particular syllabus, or putting together a set of activities. Diversity education demands a different perspective, commitment, and starting point. It is not a route lightly taken.

Effective diversity educators concentrate on authenticity and reflection. They care about equity, justice, a high quality of life for all. They struggle to reflect these in their teaching. They work in their classrooms and training sessions to offer opportunities for all to dig into the essence of life and social forces. A first question when teaching workplace diversity then is not what book or exercises to use; it is how to be more open and honest with oneself and with others. We are not advocating that educators abandon preparation or structure, adopt a "shoot from the hip" educational philosophy, or assume a Pollyannaish stance ("Just believe and all will go well"). Cases, readings, activities, and course designs need to be grounded in the kind of personal authenticity that the contributors have illustrated in this volume. All diversity-related teaching activities take on new meaning when explored openly, deeply, and honestly.

Institutional, Structural, and Systemic Issues

Identity, authenticity, and clarity about one's personal stand on the issues are essential foundations for teaching workplace diversity. A foundation is, however, a beginning, a solid base for expansion. We must not be misled into viewing diversity issues in purely interpersonal or intrapersonal terms. Diversity education begins with the individual but cannot remain there. It must explore the power of institutional, structural, and systemic forces to affect lives. In fact, this is where diversity education can make some of its strongest and most unique contributions.

Despite the importance of institutional and structural issues, there are noticeably fewer entries specifically addressing them in this volume. Our questions for and interactions with contributors may have inadvertently steered people toward the individual and interpersonal. We believe, however, that there are other factors at work as well.

Individual and interpersonal teaching and learning can be seductive. The processes are emotionally charged; the outcomes often seem more tangible. There is also potential tacit comfort for teacher and student in working on these issues. Much of Western culture values individualism. It encourages self-reflection—at least on the level of pop psychology and amateur psychoanalysis. On the whole, we are more accustomed to looking at issues and solving problems through a personal or interpersonal lens. This is true beyond diversity issues (Bolman and Deal, 1991).

Institutional issues are more challenging than individual and interpersonal ones. They feel distant and abstract. They are often difficult to isolate and untangle from intra- and interpersonal dynamics. For many of us, they are harder to get and keep a handle on. Feelings of powerlessness can also accompany increased understanding. It is easier to change oneself than to change a deeply entrenched system.

Institutional, structural, and systemic issues are very difficult for members of dominant groups to understand. Systems are most often designed by dominant group members to meet their own needs. It is then difficult to see the ways in which our institutions and structures systematically exclude others who are not "like us." It is hard to see and question what we have always taken for granted and painful to confront personal complicity in maintaining the status quo. Privilege enables us to remain unaware of institutional and social forces and their impact.

Institutional, structural, and systemic issues can also be difficult for nondominant group members, although for different reasons. Deep frustration makes it easier and quicker to confront the individual in the office next door than to take on the system. Staying at the individual and interpersonal level makes it less likely that others will charge us with overreacting or "making things up." But as the contributors make clear, facing systemic discrimination daily can be painful, dispiriting, and frustrating.

For all these reasons, institutional, structural, and systemic issues are where we most need each other—where we must try to look at the world through each other's eyes in order to identify ways in which structures and systems are exclusionary, inequitable, and damaging to individuals. Diversity education needs to make the invisible more visible at the institutional level—to make the undiscussable

discussable. It needs to reveal the dogged frustration that people feel living daily in a system not made for them and with few plans to accommodate them. Institutional and system forces are subtle yet potent. They are always present. Visible or not, acknowledged or not, structural, systemic, and institutional issues of diversity permeate all of our lives. Only knowledge and understanding of these forces can lead to needed change.

A Need to Become More Multicultural

The contributors' stories reinforced for us the need to become more multicultural. Age, religion, sexual orientation, race, ethnicity, gender, class, physical and developmental ability, and other demographic characteristics offer us unique perspectives on and experiences in the world. We need to understand better what it means to be members of various identity groups.

Members of nondominant groups have long recognized the necessity to be "bicultural." Ella Bell (1990) talks about how Black professional women effectively learn the "ways" of the dominant White culture while maintaining their own. Professional women, regardless of color, have had to learn the male model for "doing things" to survive in male-designed and -dominated organizations.

Seldom, however, have members of dominant groups—those of us who are White or male, for example—taken the time, effort, or opportunity to learn the cultures of other identity groups. It is evident, as you read the accounts throughout this volume, that once we live or work closely with members of other groups and begin to see the world through their eyes, we are forever changed. It is difficult to maintain intellectual distance when people we deeply care about are devalued simply because of a perceived "difference." It is equally hard when one has personally experienced injustice or discrimination.

More cross-cultural and multicultural experiences are essential, then, to advance diversity work. They offer opportunities to identify and question our own taken-for-granted assumptions, behaviors, and beliefs. Diversity educators need intentionally to initiate and model this. Effective diversity educators do not remain distant from what they teach.

As we advocate becoming more multicultural, we stress the importance of learning about the personal and institutional implications of all of our group memberships. Both academic and historical legacies in the United States make race and gender issues visible and obvious targets for diversity education. Women's studies and Black studies programs have peppered the liberal arts side of colleges and universities for more than two decades, generating theory and literature to advance understanding of race and gender and the intersections of the two. The civil rights movement of the 1960s and the women's movement of the 1970s placed race and gender on the national social agenda and made them natural areas of exploration for diversity teachers and learners. As a field, however, we need to think about the substantive, pedagogical, and social implications of exploring and valuing all differences. While gender and race are particularly visible, other forms of difference are equally powerful. Issues of sexual orientation, physical ability, age, religion, and socioeconomic class also affect lives but remain relatively invisible and undiscussable. It is critical for diversity educators to honor the multidimensionality of identity. We need to value this in ourselves and in others.

Finally, deep multicultural learning includes explorations of identity issues for those in dominant social groups. Too often, dominant group members attempt to learn about diversity by examining the lives of those they see as different from themselves in some way. Seeing the world through others' eyes is important but not enough. Those who are White, for example, must learn about race by understanding more about Whiteness. Learning about gender means an exploration of maleness as well as femaleness. Learning about sexual orientation requires understanding heterosexuality, and so forth. These are no small tasks for diversity educators. It is no surprise that the contributors see this as lifelong work.

The Ability and the Willingness to Embrace Paradox

A recurrent theme in this volume has been the role of paradox in diversity education. We have learned much from the contributors about this. Their stories have shown the importance of simultaneously holding on to core beliefs while letting go of rigid views of self and world. They have described modeling the confusion and muddling through that learning about diversity requires while creating a secure learning space for others. They have identified a cardinal requirement for diversity education—holding on to differences and similarities at the same time. Effective diversity education demands the ability to hold contradictions. It requires freely and passionately embracing paradox.

A critical question then becomes how effective diversity educators learn to do that. What experiences and conditions help us learn to accept and embrace contradiction? On a simple level, personal comfort and security play a role in this.

The personal comfort and security to embrace paradox come from a number of experiences and factors. Familiarity with diversity issues and dynamics is essential. We need to know the terrain. Conceptual clarity is important, as is understanding how the teaching and learning process affects both teacher and student. Feeling confident that issues and dynamics will not "blindside" us is freeing. Learning to welcome rather than avoid the unexpected helps. It enables us to relax our vigilance and release a more playful, more creative spirit.

Experience helps too. Confidence and security come from having lived through difficult teaching and learning times. After fighting a few fires, maybe even getting burned, a firefighter, for example, begins to feel confident that she knows some important things beyond book learning that will help her be more effective. Since so much of diversity teaching is ongoing learning for the instructor, diversity educators have a leg up on this issue. They know much of their own clarity came out of confusion. They have been where they are asking others to travel.

A third set of issues critical for embracing paradox is self-knowledge and self-love. When diversity educators are secure in who they are, they can accept risk and attack without peril to their basic identity. Their self-worth is not intricately tied to each exchange, interaction, or teaching moment. They can "hang loose," behaviorally, emotionally, and cognitively. They can see diversity education as an ongoing challenge, an intellectual and interpersonal puzzle that all are invited to solve. No one, not even the teacher, is expected to have the answers. Self-pride and satisfaction come from the effort.

There are also clear developmental capacities essential for embracing the paradoxes in diversity education (Gallos, 1989). A tolerance for ambiguity, acknowledgment of the social construction of knowledge, and appreciation of complexity as the norm—all essentials for holding contradictions simultaneously—are directly tied to patterns of psychological organization we refer to as stages of developmental growth. These developmental stages describe different ways of structuring one's world. Development is a slow process and results from grappling with a series of manageable challenges to one's worldview. Developmental growth leads to greater appreciation of life's paradoxes. It also implies greater capacity to acknowledge the importance of individual differences and to move beyond viewing differences as impediments to personal empowerment or effective action.

The ability to embrace paradox, however, is different from the willingness to do so. Developmental capacities speak only to educators' potential and capability. They say nothing about what they might do or if their choices will result in learning. Willingness to embrace and learn from paradox is connected to one's talent for managing levels of risk and ambiguity and identifying opportunities for informed choice. Good diversity educators know they are free to make ongoing choices about their own learning and grant that right to others. They know how to choose appropriate levels of cognitive and social confusion to produce maximum learning for themselves and others. They offer only as much complexity and contradiction as can comfortably be accepted. It is like setting the bar at a track-and-field high jump. Too high, and all fail quickly; too low, and there is no challenge.

Finally, willingness to embrace paradoxes in diversity teaching is facilitated by a bottom-line recognition that despite differences, there is an underlying unity in human existence. Difference is variation on a theme, not deviation from some norm. It is a starting point for understanding the richness of life. Diversity education is not labeling a particular group as "other" or simply learning to like people who are "different from us." It is sacred work that touches the core of what it means to be human. Differences are unique manifestations of possibilities in the human condition. No difference in age, religion, sexual orientation, race, ethnicity, gender, physical or developmental ability, or other characteristics is better or worse than any other. It just is. This does not mean that we are all the same or that we must gloss over or mask our differences. Valuing differences does not mean that we condone all behaviors or actions. It does means that in recognizing and understanding the importance of our diversity, we simultaneously acknowledge the bond of our similarities.

It is no surprise, then, that diversity education is steeped in emotion for educators and students. No one can remain dispassionate. The contributors to this volume share a wide range of feelings— love, laughter, joy, pain, anger, vulnerability, tenderness, warmth, fear, humility, timidity, confidence, self-doubt, hope, despair. They name a multitude of emotional polarities. These emotions come from deeply respecting and caring about the quality of human existence. Teaching workplace diversity is more than a job. It is a passion, a calling, a mission, a way of life.

Preparation and Faculty Development

All of the foregoing points to the need for adequate preparation for diversity educators. Little is consistently available now. On the U.S. university and professional school scene, where accreditation pressures loom, major campus discussions revolve largely around whether to have separate diversity courses or integrate diversity issues into the larger curriculum. Adequate staff training and faculty development are often overlooked or shortchanged even though the need is great.

A national study, for example, of more than three hundred management educators (Organizational Behavior Teaching Society Diversity Catalyst Group, 1993) found that although 96 percent of the respondents felt it important for students to be exposed to workplace diversity issues, only 23 percent saw present programs adequately preparing participants to deal with workplace reality. This same study found 95 percent of the respondents addressing workplace diversity issues in their own courses and classes, in most cases with self-descriptions indicating unsatisfactory or superficial treatment of the topic. The dynamics may be different in corporate settings, but budget cuts can easily substitute pressures to cover training demands for concern for competency.

Everything in this volume suggests a special kind of preparation for diversity teaching. Firm and grounded personal identity, strong knowledge of the content of the field, an understanding of how people learn, comfort and versatility in dealing with emotionally charged and potentially messy soul-work issues, the ability to teach for developmental growth and complex understanding, a realistic sense of the task, deep commitment, and a host of other competencies are needed to teach well. These must be integral to any faculty development effort, professional training, or graduate education that seeks to prepare effective diversity educators.

Preparation for diversity education is of necessity integrative. It asks educators to bring all of who they are to the work. It requires wedding the cognitive with the emotional. It explores interconnections among cognitive, socioemotional, and developmental issues for teacher and students. It examines diversity from intrapersonal, interpersonal, group, institutional, and systemic perspectives. This is an exciting and rewarding part of the work. The contributors tell us repeatedly that they develop their intellectual, emotional, and spiritual selves through, and in preparation for, their day-to-day training and classroom experiences.

The Importance of Community

Formal preparation is important. It does not, however, replace the need for a community of kindred spirits among diversity educators. From community comes learning as well as sustenance for heart and soul. The contributors to this volume relished opportunities, like this project, to expand and strengthen networks and relationships. They talked openly about the importance of community for maintaining their commitment to diversity work.

It is useful to talk about the distinctive nature of a community of like-minded souls. We have become too accustomed in management and education to thinking in instrumental terms of professional networks and contacts that further our careers. The community we advocate, however, is something more.

Communities that sustain heart and soul, in the words of poet Walt Whitman, "steer for the deep waters" ([1871] 1973, p. 284). They probe beneath the surface of thought and action. They examine the profound and intense without fear. They unabashedly question innermost beliefs. They focus on questions of *why* rather than merely asking *how*. Soulful communities encourage and enable conversations to explore purpose, identity, and all facets of life's journey. They offer support and companionship for those who struggle to understand themselves and the world. They are communities underpinned by ethics of care, learning, and love.

We are aware that using words like *care* and *love* may seem to stray from the pragmatics of education into the romantic and quixotic. We think not. As Noddings (1984) reminds us in her work on moral education, an ethic of care and love is tough-minded and practical. There is no educational arena where this is more true than diversity teaching.

Diversity educators ask tough questions. They do so within a context of concern for learners and for the overall quality of human existence. They listen for possibility—those moments when students and clients seem open and ready to delve deeper into themselves and the issues. They work with hope for new possibilities—the transformation of individual learning into a more equitable and just world. Diversity educators provide a safe haven and are there to support and encourage others in their learning. They need trusted others to do the same for them. They also need places to release the emotion and intensity that come from working on the edge of possibility. They cannot teach well or long without it.

We were moved during this project by the caring and generous spirit of the contributors. We saw this in many ways. It was evident in their good-natured responses to our requests for more or different submissions. It was most obvious, however, in how they spoke about their work and its significance. We found no attributions, attacks, or negativity toward others. We heard only repeated commitments to "do the work" they felt "called to do." They knew they could do this best in the context of a caring community of others equally committed to the task. Recurring themes—"This is work that I can best do with others," "We're all in this together," "I need foils and mirrors to learn; I am therefore willing to play those roles for others"—permeated the contributors' stories.

To our delight, the contributors found a form of this community in the book project. When we sent out drafts of the manuscript for contributors to see what we had done with their submissions, almost all reacted first to the whole rather than to their own sections. It was clear that they felt part of something bigger than themselves and even bigger than this book project. There is a special sense of community among people dedicated and committed to diversity education. There needs to be. Community is equally critical to students and clients who need others in order to learn about workplace diversity. To a large extent, what diversity educators do in their classrooms and training sessions is work to develop a community of learners.

It is a pedagogical challenge to build the classroom communities essential for diversity teaching and learning. It is often hard to see the importance of learning with and from peers. Too many educational experiences have asked us to go it alone—rewarded us for self-sufficiency and independence, denied us opportunities to develop skills in collaboration and positive interdependence. They have implicitly trained us to look to the instructor for knowledge and guidance. The intensity and personal nature of diversity education only magnifies these dynamics.

It is easier, however, for students and clients to appreciate community-based learning when they recognize the unique nature of the diversity teaching and learning process and when they clearly see how individual efforts contribute to the larger picture. Encouraging groups to generalize from individual or deeply personal learning, helping students build shared histories of their learning progress, and finding ways to develop collaborative structures all enable learners to recognize the power and educational benefits of community.

Next Steps: The Future of Diversity Education

Diversity work is in transition. What we now call diversity education, even with multiple definitions and approaches, will change as we continue to learn more about its nature and possibilities. But where are we now? And where should we go?

The contributors to this volume clearly show that the future of diversity education is in good hands. Committed, responsible, and knowledgeable educators populate the field at a time when diversity work is urgently needed to address growing ethnic and racial polarization around the globe. Globalization increases contact among groups once isolated from one another, multiplying opportunities for hatred and violence. Many still see difference as a threat, so collisions are inevitable. Worldwide needs for valuing differences and acknowledging similarities grow daily.

On the work front, demographic realities mean that differences are with us, whether we are ready and able to manage them productively or not. Marilyn Loden (1994) reminds us of the long history in the United States of viewing diversity as a liability and of "managing diversity" by overlooking or suppressing differences. Moving beyond that to seeing diversity as positive—a source of innovation and competitive advantage—poses new management and educational challenges.

On the academic scene, students and accreditation pressures force institutions to change. Universities turn to diversity issues, often with hesitation, as a means to making education "relevant" for those who prepare for life and work in a global society. Growing recognition of the importance of diversity education on multiple fronts is opening greater opportunities and possibilities for the field.

Throughout this book, we have referred to diversity education as a field or a discipline. To some extent, we assumed poetic license. The expression "teaching workplace diversity" is an umbrella for a wide range of issues, practices, purposes, and events. Diversity education needs to be diverse, but it also needs integration, clarity, and connection.

Diversity education needs to take stock of itself and build a home. The time is right for its full recognition as a distinct area of study and practice rather than an offshoot of management education, cross-cultural studies, organizational development, women's studies, Black studies, ethnic studies, and so on. Diversity issues have broad implications for a wide range of fields. It must, however, acknowledge and integrate the many strands, contributions, splinters, and side roads that, like diversity itself, add richness, perspective, and depth to the issues. It must stand proud and firm as a multidisciplinary endeavor and chart its own future development and direction.

This volume identifies critical areas for future research and study. There is more we still need to know about diversity teaching and learning. How do we best learn about complex and deeply personal issues like diversity? What are the internal learning processes for individuals? What are the pedagogical options for instructors? What do effective diversity educators need to learn about learning in order to teach well? How can we learn these things best?

Thinking about how to learn about workplace diversity raises parallel questions of when and where to explore the issues. It asks us to look at implicit assumptions about educational arenas. Education about workplace diversity most often occurs today in corporations or universities and professional schools and focuses on adults. This means relatively little dialogue and exchange with educators who do diversity teaching in elementary and secondary schools. The complexity and difficulty of the issues suggest that learning needs to be take place incrementally over long periods of time. The present adult-centered focus of workplace diversity education leads to missed opportunities for developing a philosophy of teaching and learning about workplace diversity across the life span.

This suggests new linkages and connections among diversity educators. It means expanding the present scope of diversity education and developing more integrated methods for teaching and learning at all life stages. We need greater understanding of the educational needs that different-aged students bring to diversity work and of the developmental capabilities needed for diversity learning at those different ages and stages.

This volume also points to a need for developing better structures and institutional conditions to support diversity teaching and learning. One obvious area for attention is evaluation. Diversity teaching success cannot be measured over the short term. Diversity learning takes time, experience, and personal integration. Diversity educators all have stories of students who hated particular courses, classes, or workshops yet reported these events months or years later as powerful sources of personal learning or as a major impetus for institutional change. Course and workshop evaluations, though helpful for instructors to learn about the immediate impact of their methods, are of limited value as institutional measures of instructor competency or teaching success. Measures of longer-term impact need to become an integral feature of diversity education.

If diversity education is to be a legitimate, multidisciplinary endeavor, its institutional locus becomes important. Content and process knowledge for diversity education come from a number of disciplines. How can diversity education benefit from these diverse sources? How can it grow and develop as a field, managing productively the internal and ideological battles that other evolving multidisciplinary fields have experienced?

The history of organizational behavior, for example, is filled with conflict among scholars rooted in different discipline-based perspectives or frameworks: psychologists defining the field in micro and individual terms, sociologists designating the turf as group and institutional issues, political scientists claiming preeminence for systemic power-related dynamics, anthropologists asserting cultural issues as the name of the game. If diversity education is to learn from the experiences of other multidisciplinary fields, it needs to develop within the context of its own teachings. It would be ironic and especially sad if diversity education were to be torn apart by issues of difference.

Finally, diversity education as a field needs to evolve with equal appreciation for all differences and for what might be called the "generic versus local" tension in learning about difference. Age, race, ethnicity, gender, sexual orientation, class, physical or developmental abilities, and other differences each bring unique sets of issues, rhythms, and dynamics to the learning table. It would be foolish to assume that one understands race, for example, by having explored issues of gender, and vice versa. There are nevertheless similarities in the two sets of issues—dynamics of oppression, for example—that Barry Oshry (1995) reminds us have been played out among people throughout the millennia. An ability to hold both the uniqueness and the similarities in exploring differences is critical for the evolution of the field.

A Few Simple Truths

This book set out to explore teaching workplace diversity. It asked experienced diversity educators to listen to their souls and speak from their hearts so that others might understand the joys and challenges in the educational task. The contributors have done this well. We thank them for their hard work and candor.

We end this project, however, surprising ourselves. Rather than close with reminders of the complexities in all this, we find ourselves wanting to share a few simple truths. Despite all we have discussed about process and content, teaching and learning, choices and options, people and institutions, there is something profoundly simple about workplace diversity education. It is the honest meeting of minds, hearts, and souls. It is human beings, in all their glory and frailty, traveling together on a voyage of mutual discovery. No big deal if we take a wrong turn. In fact, the detour might be glorious. No need to plan every minute of the journey. Traveling to new places is hard work: it's nice to rest and coast sometimes. We can't alter the time it takes to get where we're going by repeatedly asking, "Are we there yet?" We might as well relax and enjoy the companionship and the journey.

Sources on Diversity

In recommending resources on diversity, we saw merit in drawing on the experience of all who contributed to this volume. We asked contributors to identify five to ten sources that have been powerful influences on their own teaching and learning about diversity. We also requested a list of their own published works on diversity-related issues. We included our recommendations and publications as well. The result is what you see—a rich and wonderfully eclectic set of resources on diversity. May these assist you on your diversity journey, suggest new side roads, and introduce unexplored territory.

Allport, G. W. *The Nature of Prejudice*. New York: Anchor Books, 1958.

American Association of University Women. *How Schools Shortchange Girls*. Washington, D.C.: AAUW Educational Foundation/National Education Association, 1992.

Amir, Y. "Contact Hypothesis in Ethnic Relations." *Psychological Bulletin*, 1969, *11*, 319–342.

Anderson, M. L., and Collins, P. H. (eds.). *Race, Class, and Gender: An Anthology*. Belmont, Calif.: Wadsworth, 1992.

Angelou, M. *I Know Why the Caged Bird Sings*. New York: Bantam Books, 1993.

Banet, A. G., Jr. "Yin/Yang: A Perspective on Theories of Group Development." In J. W. Pfeiffer and J. E. Jones (eds.), *Annual Handbook of Group Facilitators*. La Jolla, Calif.: University Associates, 1976.

Belenky, M. F., Clinchy, B. M., Goldberger, N. R., and Tarule, J. M. *Women's Ways of Knowing: The Development of Self, Voice, and Mind*. New York: Basic Books, 1986.

Bell, E. L. "The Bicultural Life Experience of Career-Oriented Black Women." *Journal of Organizational Behavior,* 1990, *11,* 459–477.

Bell, E. L., Denton, T., and Nkomo, S. "Women of Color in Management: Toward an Inclusive Analysis." In *Women in Management: Trends, Issues and Challenges in Managerial Diversity.* Thousand Oaks, Calif.: Sage, 1993.

Betters-Reed, B. L. *Toward Transformation of the Management Curriculum: Visions and Voices for Inclusion.* Working Paper Series, no. 269. Wellesley, Mass.: Center for Research on Women, Wellesley College, 1994.

Betters-Reed, B. L., and Moore, L. L. "Managing Diversity in Organizations: Professional and Curricular Issues." *Organizational Behavior Teaching Review,* 1988–1989, *13*(4), 25–32.

Betters-Reed, B. L., and Moore, L. L. "Managing Diversity: Focusing on Women and the Whitewash Dilemma." In U. Sekaran and F. Leong (eds.), *Womanpower: Managing in Times of Demographic Turbulence.* Thousand Oaks, Calif.: Sage, 1991.

Betters-Reed, B. L., and Moore, L. L. "The Technicolor Workplace." *Ms.,* Nov.-Dec. 1992, pp. 84–85.

Betters-Reed, B. L., and Moore, L. L. "Shifting the Management Development Paradigm for Women." *Journal of Management Development,* 1995, *14*(2), 24–38.

Betters-Reed, B. L., and Moore, L. L. "Women Entrepreneurs." In P. J. Dubeck and K. Borman (eds.), *Women and Work: A Handbook.* New York: Garland, 1996.

Blau, P. *Inequality and Heterogeneity.* New York: Free Press, 1977.

Boje, D. M. "Stories of the Storytelling Organization: A Postmodern Analysis of Disney as "Tamara-land." *Academy of Management Journal,* 1995, *38,* 997–1035.

Boje, D. M., and Dennehy, R. *Managing in the Postmodern World: America's Revolution Against Exploitation.* Dubuque, Iowa: Kendall/Hunt, 1993.

Boje, D. M., Gephart, J., and Thatchenkery, T. *Postmodern Management and Organizational Theory.* Thousand Oaks, Calif.: Sage, 1996.

Boje, D. M., and Rosile, G. A. "Diversities, Differences and Authors' Voices." *Journal of Organizational Change Management,* 1994, *7*(6), 8–17.

Boje, D. M., White, J., and Wolfe, T. "The Consultant's Dilemma: A Multiple Frame Analysis of a Public Housing Community." In R. W. Woodman and B. Passmore (eds.), *Research in Organizational Change and Development,* Vol. 8. Greenwich, Conn.: JAI Press, 1994.

Brannon, R. "Dimensions of the Male Sex Role in America." In A. Sargent (ed.), *Beyond Sex Roles.* St. Paul, Minn.: West, 1984.

Calas, M. B., and Smircich, L. "Using the 'F' Word: Feminist Theories and the Social Consequences of Organizational Research." In A. J. Mills and P. Tancred (eds.), *Gendering Organizational Analysis*. Thousand Oaks, Calif.: Sage, 1992.

Calvert, L. M., and Ramsey, V. J. "Bringing Women's Voice to Research on Women in Management." *Journal of Management Inquiry*, 1992, *1*(1), 79–88.

Chan, S. *Asian Americans: An Interpretive History*. Old Tappan, N.J.: Twayne, 1991.

Cheng, C. "Diversity as Community and Communion: A Taoist Alternative to Modernity." *Journal of Organizational Change Management*, 1994, *7*(6), 49–58.

Cheng, C. "Multileveled Gender Conflict Analysis and Organizational Change." *Journal of Organizational Change Management*, 1995, *8*(5), 26–57.

Cheng, C. "The 'Good Manager' Ideal Type as a Hegemonically Masculine and Orientalist Discourse of Racial Discrimination Against Asian and Asian-American Men: Deconstructing the Organizational Defensiveness of the 'Merit' Discourse in the Selection Process." In C. Cheng (ed.), *Masculinities and Organizations*. Thousand Oaks, Calif.: Sage, 1996.

Chodorow, N. J. *Feminism and Psychoanalytic Theory*. New Haven, Conn.: Yale University Press, 1989.

Cole, J. B. "Commonalities and Differences." In J. B. Cole (ed.), *All-American Women: Lines That Divide, Ties That Bind*. New York: Free Press, 1986.

Collins, P. H. *Black Feminist Thought: Knowledge, Consciousness, and the Politics of Empowerment*. Boston: Unwin Hyman, 1990.

Comnenou, C. "The Bilingual Program and Its Environment: Balancing Critical Interactions." In G. De George (ed.), *Bilingual Program Management*. Cambridge, Mass.: Evaluation, Dissemination and Assessment Center, Lesley College, 1985.

Comnenou, C. "Cross-Cultural Transitions Training for Professional Preparation: An Integrated Model." Unpublished doctoral dissertation, University of Massachusetts, 1991.

Cox, T., Jr. "The Multicultural Organization." *Academy of Management Executive*, 1991, *5*(2), 34–47.

Cox, T., Jr. *Cultural Diversity in Organizations: Theory, Research and Practice*. San Francisco: Berrett-Koehler, 1993.

Cox, T., Jr., and Nkomo, S. M. "Invisible Men and Women: A Status Report on Race as a Variable in Organization Behavior Research." *Journal of Organizational Behavior*, 1990, *11*, 419–431.

Davis, A. *Women, Race, and Class*. New York: Random House, 1983.

Davis, F. J. *Who Is Black? One Nation's Definition*. University Park, Pa.: Pennsylvania University Press, 1991.

Delpit, L. D. *Other People's Children: Cultural Conflict in the Classroom*. New York: New Press, 1995.

Derrida, J. *Of Grammatology* (G. C. Spivak, trans.). Baltimore: Johns Hopkins University Press, 1976.

Derrida, J. *Writing and Difference* (A. Bass, trans.). Chicago: University of Chicago Press, 1978.

Duneier, M. *Slim's Table: Race, Respectability, and Masculinity*. Chicago: University of Chicago Press, 1992.

Estes, C. P. *Women Who Run with the Wolves: Myths and Stories of the Wild Woman Archetype*. New York: Ballantine, 1992.

Fanon, F. *The Wretched of the Earth* (C. Farrington, trans.). New York: Ballantine, 1963.

Fanon, F. *Black Skin, White Masks*. New York: Grove Press, 1967.

Farganis, S. *Situating Feminism: From Thought to Action*, Vol. 2: *Contemporary Social Theory*. Thousand Oaks, Calif.: Sage, 1994.

Ferguson, K. E. *The Feminist Case Against Bureaucracy*. Philadelphia: Temple University Press, 1984.

Flax, J. *Thinking Fragments: Psychoanalysis, Feminism, and Postmodernism in the Contemporary West*. Berkeley: University of California Press, 1990.

Frankenburg, R. *The Social Construction of Whiteness: White Women, Race Matters*. Minneapolis: University of Minnesota Press, 1993.

Freire, P. *Pedagogy of the Oppressed* (M. B. Ramos, trans.). New York: Continuum, 1990.

Freire, P. *Education for Critical Consciousness* (M. B. Ramos, trans.). New York: Continuum, 1992.

Frye, M. "On Being White: Toward a Feminist Understanding of Race and Race Supremacy." In M. Frye (ed.), *The Politics of Reality: Essays in Feminist Theory*. Freedom, Calif.: Crossing Press, 1983.

Gallos, J. V. "Developmental Diversity and the OB Classroom: Implications for Teaching and Learning." *Organizational Behavior Teaching Review*, 1989, *13*(4), 33–47.

Gallos, J. V. "Exploring Women's Development: Implications for Career Theory, Practice, and Research." In M. Arthur, D. Hall, and B. Lawrence (eds.), *Handbook of Career Theory: Perspectives and Prospects for Understanding and Managing Work Experiences*. Cambridge: Cambridge University Press, 1989.

Gallos, J. V. "Educating Women and Men in the Twenty-First Century: Gender Diversity, Leadership Opportunities." *Journal of Continuing Higher Education*, 1992, 40(1), 2–8.

Gallos, J. V. "Developmental Diversity and the Management Classroom: Implications for Teaching and Learning." In C. Vance (ed.), *Mastering Management Education: Innovations in Teaching Effectiveness*. Thousand Oaks, Calif.: Sage, 1993.

Gallos, J. V. "Understanding the Organizational Behavior Classroom: An Application of Developmental Theory." *Journal of Management Education*, 1993, 17(4), 423–439.

Gallos, J. V. "Women's Experiences and Ways of Knowing: Implications for Teaching and Learning in the Organizational Behavior Classroom." *Journal of Management Education*, 1993, 17(1), 7–26.

Gallos, J. V. "Gender and Silence: The Implications of Women's Ways of Knowing for Effective College Teaching." *College Teaching*, 1995, 43(3), 101–105.

Gallos, J. V. "On Management Education for Women: Faulty Assumptions, New Possibilities." *Selections*, Winter 1995, pp. 24–31.

Gallos, J. V. "When Authority = She: A Male Student Meets a Female Instructor." *Journal of Management Development*, 1995, 14(2), 76–86.

Gallos, J. V. "Women's Adult Development." In P. J. Dubeck and K. Borman (eds.), *Women and Work: A Handbook*. New York: Garland, 1996.

Gentile, M. *Ways of Thinking About and Across Difference*. Boston: Harvard Business School, 1995.

Gergen, M. M. (ed.). *Feminist Thought and the Structure of Knowledge*. New York: New York University Press, 1988.

Giddings, P. *When and Where I Enter: The Impact of Black Women on Race and Sex in America*. New York: Morrow, 1984.

Gillespie, J., and Meyer, G. W. "Gender, Voice, Electronic Communication and Postmodern Values: Beyond E-Mail to E-Talk." *Journal of Organizational Change Management*, 1995, 8(2), 29–44.

Gilligan, C. *In a Different Voice: Psychological Theory and Women's Development*. Cambridge, Mass.: Harvard University Press, 1982.

Grant, J. "Women as Managers: What They Can Offer to Organizations." *Organizational Dynamics*, 1988, 16(3), 56–63.

Gwaltney, J. L. *Drylongso: A Self-Portrait of Black Americans*. New York: Random House, 1980.

Hacker, A. *Two Nations: Black and White, Separate, Hostile, Unequal*. New York: Scribner, 1992.

Hamper, B. *Rivethead: Tales from the Assembly Line*. New York: Warner Books, 1991.

Harding, S. *Whose Science? Whose Knowledge?* Ithaca, N.Y.: Cornell University Press, 1991.

Harvey, J. "Encouraging Students to Cheat: One Thought on the Difference Between Teaching Ethics and Teaching Ethically." *Organizational Behavior Teaching Review*, 1984, 9(2), 1–13.

Helgesen, S. *The Female Advantage: Women's Ways of Leadership*. New York: Doubleday, 1990.

Holvina, E. "Women of Color in Organizations." In E. Y. Cross, J. H. Katz, F. A. Miller, and E. W. Seashore (eds.), *The Promise of Diversity*. Burr Ridge, Ill.: Irwin, 1994.

hooks, b. *Ain't I a Woman? Black Women and Feminism*. Boston: South End Press, 1981.

hooks, b. *Feminist Theory: From Margin to Center*. Boston: South End Press, 1984.

hooks, b. *Talking Back: Thinking Feminist, Thinking Black*. Boston: South End Press, 1989.

hooks, b. *Yearning: Race, Gender and Cultural Politics*. Boston: South End Press, 1990.

Illich, I. *Tools for Conviviality*. San Francisco: Harper San Francisco, 1973.

Jackson, B. *Stages of Black Identity Development*. Amherst: School of Education, University of Massachusetts, 1978.

Jones, M. C. "A Contribution or a Commitment? Personal Insights on Diversity Appreciation in the Classroom." *Journal of Management Education*, 1994, 18, 432–437.

Jordan, W. D. *White over Black: American Attitudes Toward the Negro, 1550–1812*. Chapel Hill: University of North Carolina Press, 1968.

Juffer, K. A. "Initial Development and Assessment of an Instrument to Assess the Degree of Culture Shock Adaptation." Unpublished doctoral dissertation, University of Iowa, 1983.

Kanter, R. M. *Men and Women of the Corporation*. New York: Basic Books, 1977.

Kegan, R. *In Over Our Heads: The Mental Demands of Modern Life*. Cambridge, Mass.: Harvard University Press, 1994.

Kellogg, D. M., and Moore, L. L. "Teaching Undergraduate Women in Management Courses: Issues and Ideas." In V. J. Ramsey (ed.), *Preparing Professional Women for the Future: Resources for Teachers and Trainers*. Ann Arbor: Division of Research, Graduate School of Business Administration, University of Michigan, 1985.

Kellogg, D. M., Spelman, D., and Crary, M. "Introducing Women in Management Issues in an OB Course." *Organizational Behavior Teaching Review*, 1984–1985, 9(3), 83–95.

Kirkham, K. "Teaching About Diversity: Navigating the Emotional Undercurrents." *Organizational Behavior Teaching Review*, 1989, 13(4), 48–55.

Kolb, D. A. *Experiential Learning: Experience as the Source of Learning and Development*. Upper Saddle River, N.J.: Prentice Hall, 1984.

Kovel, J. *White Racism: A Psychohistory*. New York: Columbia University Press, 1984.

La Fromboise, T., Coleman, H.L.K., and Gerton, J. "Psychological Impact of Biculturalism: Evidence and Theory." *Psychological Bulletin*, 1993, 114, 395–412.

Lee, D. *Freedom and Culture*. Upper Saddle River, N.J.: Prentice Hall, 1956.

Lee, D. *Valuing the Self: What We Can Learn from Other Cultures*. Upper Saddle River, N.J.: Prentice Hall, 1976.

Lee, J. *At My Father's Wedding*. New York: Bantam Books, 1992.

Lewin, K. "Field Theory in Social Science." In D. Cartright (ed.), *Field Theory in Social Science: Selected Theoretical Papers*. New York: HarperCollins, 1951.

Lobber, J., and Farrell, S. (eds.). *The Social Construction of Gender*. Thousand Oaks, Calif.: Sage, 1991.

Lorde, A. *Sister Outsider*. Freedom, Calif.: Crossing Press, 1984.

Lyotard, J. *The Postmodern Condition: A Report on Knowledge* (G. Bennington and B. Massumi, trans.). Minneapolis: University of Minnesota Press, 1984.

Marable, M. *How Capitalism Underdeveloped Black America*. Boston: South End Press, 1983.

Martin, J., and Knopoff, K. "The Gendered Implications of Apparently Gender-Neutral Theory: Rereading Weber." In E. Freeman and A. Larson (eds.), *Business Ethics and Women's Studies*, Vol. 3. Oxford: Oxford University Press, 1996.

Mayes, N., and Comnenou, C. "Teacher Training for Cultural Awareness." *Overview of Intercultural Education Training and Research*. Pittsburgh: Society for Intercultural Education, Training and Research, 1978.

McIntosh, P. "White Privilege and Male Privilege: Unpacking the Invisible Knapsack." In M. L. Andersen and P. H. Collins (eds.), *Race, Class, and Gender: An Anthology*. Belmont, Calif.: Wadsworth, 1992.

Miller, J. B. *Toward a New Psychology of Women*. Boston: Beacon Press, 1986.

Moore, L. L. (ed.). *Not as Far as You Think: The Realities of Working Women*. San Francisco: New Lexington Press, 1986.

Moraga, C., and Anzaldua, G. (eds.). *This Bridge Called My Back: Writings by*

Radical Women of Color. New York: Kitchen Table/Women of Color Press, 1983.

Morrison, A. M. *The New Leaders: Guidelines on Leadership Diversity in America.* San Francisco: Jossey-Bass, 1992.

Morrison, A. M., Ruderman, M. M., and Hughes-James, M. *Making Diversity Happen: Controversies and Solutions.* Greensboro, N.C.: Center for Creative Leadership, 1993.

Morrison, A. M., and Von Glinow, M. A. "Women and Minorities in Management." *American Psychologist,* 1990, *45,* 200–208.

Morrison, A. M., White, R. P., and Van Velsor, E. *Breaking the Glass Ceiling: Can Women Reach the Top of America's Largest Corporations?* Reading, Mass.: Addison-Wesley, 1992.

Mumby, D. K., and Putnam, L. "'Bounded Rationality' and Organizing: A Feminist Critique." *Academy of Management Review,* 1992, *17,* 465–486.

Newman, K. S. *Falling from Grace: The Experience of Downward Mobility in the American Middle Class.* New York: Free Press, 1988.

Nkomo, S. M. "Race and Sex: The Forgotten Case of the Black Female Manager." In S. Rose and L. Larwood (eds.), *Women's Careers: Pathways and Pitfalls.* New York: Praeger, 1988.

Nkomo, S. M. "The Emperor Has No Clothes: Rewriting 'Race in Organizations.'" *Academy of Management Review,* 1992, *17,* 487–513.

Palmer, J. D. "Stages of Women's Awareness." *Social Change,* 1979, *9*(1).

Pleck, J. "Men's Power with Women, Other Men, and Society: A Men's Movement Analysis." In E. Peck and J. Peck (eds.), *The American Man.* Upper Saddle River, N.J.: Prentice Hall, 1980.

Pratt, M. B. "Identity: Skin Blood Heart." In E. Bulkin, M. B. Pratt, and B. Smith (eds.), *Yours in Struggle: Three Feminist Perspectives on Anti-Semitism and Racism.* Ithaca, N.Y.: Firebrand, 1984.

Ramsey, V. J. *Preparing Professional Women for the Future: Resources for Teachers and Trainers.* Ann Arbor: Division of Research, Graduate School of Business Administration, University of Michigan, 1985.

Ramsey, V. J. "A Different Way of Making a Difference: Learning Through Feelings." *Journal of Organizational Change Management,* 1994, *7*(6), 59–71.

Ramsey, V. J. "'Evenhandedness' in Workforce Diversity Courses." *Journal of Management Education,* 1994, *18,* 424–427.

Ramsey, V. J., and Calvert, L. M. "A Feminist Critique of Organizational Humanism." *Journal of Applied Behavioral Science,* 1994, *30*(1), 98–102.

Sadler, M., and Sadker, D. *Failing at Fairness: How America's Schools Cheat Girls.* New York: Scribner, 1994.

Said, E. W. *Orientalism*. New York: Pantheon, 1978.

Sandler, B. "Project Status and the Education of Women." *Commentary*, *81*(1), 13–14.

Schaef, A. W. *Women's Reality: An Emerging Female System in a White Male Society*. San Francisco: Harper San Francisco, 1985.

Schein, E. H. *Organizational Culture and Leadership*. (2nd ed.) San Francisco: Jossey-Bass, 1992.

Schrank, R. "Two Women, Three Men on a Raft." *Harvard Business Review*, May-June 1994, pp. 68–80.

Scott, J. W. "Deconstructing Equality-Versus-Difference: Or, the Uses of Post-structuralist Theory for Feminism." *Feminist Studies*, 1988, *14*(1), 33–49.

Sekaran, U., and Leong, F. *Womanpower: Managing in Times of Demographic Turbulence*. Thousand Oaks, Calif.: Sage, 1992.

Spelman, D. "White Men and Managing Diversity." *Diversity Factor*, Spring 1993, pp. 8–15.

Spelman, D. "Our Roles as Teachers of Diversity." *Journal of Management Education*, 1994, *18*, 438–440.

Spelman, D., and Crary, M. "Intimacy or Distance? A Case on Male-Female Attraction at Work." *Organizational Behavior Teaching Review*, 1984, 9(2), 72–85.

Spelman, D., Crary, M., Kram, K., and Clawson, J. "Sexual Attraction at Work: Managing the Heart." In L. L. Moore (ed.), *Not as Far as You Think: The Realities of Working Women*. San Francisco: New Lexington Press, 1986.

Spelman, D., Crary, M., Weathersby, R., and Boccialetti, G. "Men Students in Women and Management Courses: Learnings and Dilemmas." *Organizational Behavior Teaching Review*, 1985–1986, *10*(4), 89–97.

Stewart, E. C., Danielian, J., and Foster, G. M. "Simulating Intercultural Communication Through Role Playing." In D. S. Hoopes and P. Ventura (eds.), *Intercultural Sourcebook: Cross-Cultural Training Methodologies*. Chicago: Intercultural Press, 1979.

Tepper, S. S. *The Gate to Women's Country*. New York: Bantam Books, 1989.

Thomas, R., Jr. *Beyond Race and Gender*. New York: American Management Association, 1991.

Thomson, R. G. "Integrating Disability Studies into the Existing Curriculum: The Example of 'Women and Literature' at Howard University." *Radical Teacher*, 1995, *47*, 15–21.

Trickett, E. J., Watts, R. J., and Birman, D. (eds.). *Human Diversity: Perspectives on People in Context*. San Francisco: Jossey-Bass, 1994.

Tsui, A. S., Egan, T. D., & O'Reilly, C. A., III. "Being Different: Relational

Demography and Organizational Attachment." *Administrative Science Quarterly*, 1992, 37, 549–579.

Walker, A. *In Search of Our Mothers' Gardens: Womanist Prose*. Orlando, Fla.: Harcourt Brace, 1983.

Walker, A. *Possessing the Secret of Joy*. Orlando, Fla.: Harcourt Brace, 1992.

Walker, B. A. "Valuing Differences." Paper presented at the annual meeting of the Academy of Management, Washington, D.C., August 1989.

Walker, B. A. "How the Valuing Differences Approach Evolved at Digital Equipment Corporation." In M. A. Smith and S. J. Johnson (eds.), *Valuing Differences in the Workplace*. Alexandria, Va.: American Society for Training and Development, 1991.

Walker, B. A. "Valuing Differences: The Concept and a Model." In M. A. Smith and S. J. Johnson (eds.), *Valuing Differences in the Workplace*. Alexandria, Va.: American Society for Training and Development, 1991.

Walker, B. A., and Hanson, W. C. "Valuing Differences at Digital Equipment Corporation." In S. E. Jackson and Associates (eds.), *Diversity in the Workplace: Human Resources Initiatives*. New York: Guilford Press, 1992.

West, C. *Race Matters*. New York: Vintage Books, 1994.

Wilson, E. O. *The Diversity of Life*. Cambridge, Mass.: Harvard University Press, 1992.

Wood, F. G. *Arrogance of Faith: Christianity and Race in America from the Colonial Era to the Twentieth Century*. New York: Knopf, 1990.

Woodman, M. *The Pregnant Virgin: A Process of Psychological Transformation*. Toronto: Inner City Books, 1985.

Wurzel, J. S. (ed.). *Toward Multiculturalism*. Yarmouth, Maine: Intercultural Press, 1988.

Yalom, I. D. *Existential Psychotherapy*. New York: Basic Books, 1980.

Zanardi, C. (ed.). *Essential Papers on the Psychology of Women*. New York: New York University Press, 1990.

References

Argyris, C., and Schön, D. A. *Theory in Practice: Increasing Professional Effectiveness*. San Francisco: Jossey-Bass, 1974.

Bell, E. L. "The Bicultural Life Experience of Career-Oriented Black Women." *Journal of Organizational Behavior*, 1990, *11*, 459–477.

Bolman, L. G., and Deal, T. E. *Reframing Organizations: Artistry, Choice, and Leadership*. San Francisco: Jossey-Bass, 1991.

Braverman, H. *Labor and Monopoly Capital: The Degradation of Work in the Twentieth Century*. New York: Monthly Review Press, 1974.

Cary, L. *Black Ice*. New York: Knopf, 1991.

Cole, J. B. "Commonalities and Differences." In J. B. Cole (ed.), *All-American Women: Lines That Divide, Ties That Bind*. New York: Free Press, 1986.

Collins, P. H. *Black Feminist Thought: Knowledge, Consciousness, and the Politics of Empowerment*. Boston: Unwin Hyman, 1990.

Cose, E. *The Rage of a Privileged Class*. New York: HarperCollins, 1993.

Cox, T., Jr. *Cultural Diversity in Organizations: Theory, Research, and Practice*. San Francisco: Berrett-Koehler, 1993.

Edwards, R. C. *Contested Terrain: The Transformation of the Workplace in the Twentieth Century*. New York: Basic Books, 1979.

Freire, P. *Pedagogy of the Oppressed* (M. B. Ramos, trans.). New York: Continuum, 1990.

Gallos, J. V. "Developmental Diversity and the OB Classroom: Implications for Teaching and Learning." *Organizational Behavior Teaching Review*, 1989, *13*(4), 33–47.

Giddings, P. *When and Where I Enter: The Impact of Black Women on Race and Sex in America*. New York: Morrow, 1984.

Hall, R. M., and Sandler, B. R. *The Classroom Climate: A Chilly One for Women?* Washington, D.C.: Project on the Status and Education of Women, Association of American Colleges, 1982.

Hennig, M., and Jardim, A. *The Managerial Woman.* New York: Anchor Books, 1977.

hooks, b. *Feminist Theory: From Margin to Center.* Boston: South End Press, 1984.

hooks, b. *Talking Back: Thinking Feminist, Thinking Black.* Boston: South End Press, 1989.

Illich, I. *Deschooling Society.* New York: HarperCollins, 1971.

Kolb, D. A. *Experiential Learning: Experience as the Source of Learning and Development.* Upper Saddle River, N.J.: Prentice Hall, 1984.

Loden, M. "Diversity Management: The Challenge of Change." In E. Y. Cross, J. H. Katz, F. A. Miller, and E. W. Seashore (eds.), *The Promise of Diversity.* Burr Ridge, Ill.: Irwin, 1994.

Lorde, A. *Sister Outsider.* Freedom, Calif.: Crossing Press, 1984.

Moore, T. *Care of the Soul.* New York: HarperCollins, 1992.

Noddings, N. *Caring: A Feminine Approach to Ethics and Moral Education.* Berkeley: University of California Press, 1984.

Norton, D. L., and Kille, M. F. *Philosophies of Love.* Novato, Calif.: Chandler & Sharp, 1971.

Organizational Behavior Teaching Society Diversity Catalyst Group. *Survey of Participants in the 1991 Organizational Behavior Teaching Conference on Issues of Diversity in Management Education.* Unpublished manuscript, 1993.

Oshry, B. *Seeing Systems.* San Francisco: Berrett-Koehler, 1995.

Parker, P. *Movement in Black.* Ithaca, N.Y.: Firebrand Books, 1978.

Schaef, A. W. *Women's Reality: An Emerging Female System in a White Male Society.* San Francisco: Harper San Francisco, 1981.

Tomaskovic-Devey, T. *Race, Ethnic and Gender Earnings Inequality: The Source and Consequences of Employment Segregation.* Washington, D.C.: U.S. Department of Labor, Glass Ceiling Commission, 1994.

Vontress, C. "Cultural Barriers in the Counseling Relationships." In P. Pedersen (ed.), *Readings in Intercultural Communication,* Vol. 4: *Cross-Cultural Counseling.* Washington, D.C.: Society for Intercultural Education, Research and Training, 1975.

Walker, B. A., and Hanson, W. C. "Valuing Differences at Digital Equipment Corporation." In S. E. Jackson and Associates (eds.), *Diversity in the Workplace: Human Resources Initiatives.* New York: Guilford Press, 1992.

Watts, A. *The Book*. New York: Vintage Books, 1966.

Whitman, W. "Passage to India." In M. Van Doren (ed.), *The Portable Walt Whitman*. New York: Viking Penguin, 1973. (Originally published 1871.)

Wright, J. P. *On a Clear Day You Can See General Motors*. New York: Avon, 1979.

The Editors

JOAN V. GALLOS is Associate Professor in the Division of Urban Leadership and Policy Studies in Education, School of Education, University of Missouri–Kansas City, where she explores issues of teaching, learning, and professional effectiveness. Raised in a tight-knit ethnic community in New Jersey, Gallos was educated in parochial schools, obtained her B.A. degree in English at Princeton, cum laude, and earned Ed.M. and Ed.D. degrees, with a concentration in organizational theory and behavior, at Harvard. She is editor of the *Journal of Management Education*, a dedicated wife and mother of two sons, a member of the board of directors of the Organizational Behavior Teaching Society, an avid dog lover and Dalmatian owner, and a member of the national steering committee for the joint American Assembly of Collegiate Schools of Business–Graduate Management Admission Council "new models of management education" project. When she is not teaching, reading books with children, or fantasizing about her comeback as a cabaret singer, Gallos can be found at her computer writing passionately about the art and craft of good teaching.

V. JEAN RAMSEY lives in Houston, Texas, and is on the faculty of the Jesse H. Jones School of Business at Texas Southern University. Her earlier pursuits included degrees from New Mexico State

University and the University of Michigan, and several teaching and administrative positions at Western Michigan University and Illinois State University. Ramsey is, however, most attuned to and delighted with her present life. Students and colleagues are her forthright, challenging, provocative, loving, and patient "teachers," helping her accomplish her goal of "love, laughter, and learning" inside and outside of the classroom. Other wonderful friends and family members add to her current enjoyment of life.

The Contributors

A Note from the Contributors

Joan Gallos and Jean Ramsey set out to do something different. How wonderfully different it has been for us all! We have been part of a chorus of voices. It has enriched us in unanticipated ways.

Writing authentic, personal narratives has been both frightening and empowering. We heard the gentle invocation to be open and honest. We had confidence that being "in process" was acceptable, even valued, as part of this human endeavor called exploring diversity teaching and learning. The freedom to write in fragments—chunks and nodes, as one contributor put it—made it easier to be open. We could feel safely vulnerable in our "unfinishedness," knowing that our words would be interwoven with those of trusted others.

It can be powerfully unsettling and scary, yet energizing, to write authentically and reflexively, knowing that the words will be read by strangers and friends. Many of us were writing for the first time about our professional and personal identities and our feelings about them. As one contributor noted, "We walk around carrying stories that we think no one wants to hear or no one else even remotely shares. We aren't quite certain how we might tell them—or even if we should. Then something like this book happens, which opens the floodgate of our inner selves."

The experience of telling our individual stories, however, has helped us discover new faith in ourselves. It has renewed our commitment to continued learning. It has reminded us again of the power of faith that others have in us. Many of us now have a better sense of our own voices. We have been emboldened by and in our work. We have learned much.

In the process of writing, we have also developed an appreciation for the role of mundane and everyday occurrences in our learning. As one contributor noted: "Writing for this book was itself a marvelous process of learning about diversity. Trying to be aware of learning experiences caused me to watch for and grasp more of the day-to-day things that, in the busyness of other teaching and learning, might have gone unnoticed. I now believe that we learn far more from the day-to-day—every day, month, and year—learning experiences than from formal 'diversity training' sessions."

New and deeper connections were made with fellow travelers. Another of us wrote: "I feel as if I've found a new branch of extended family. And what a wonderful group of 'siblings' I have! I just want to say thanks to each of you for going so deeply, honestly, and fully into your souls and to Jean and Joan for taking these precious pieces of ourselves and so lovingly weaving them into a beautiful quilt. The result is that each swatch has its own texture and history. The stitching to various other pieces makes each a source of comfort for us and many others."

We have been humbled when reading the contributions of others. We have also been drawn together in new ways. The passion is so evident. The stories are so rich, real, and honest that we are now bonded to each other—even though some of us have never met. Images of the sacred keep recurring in our words and thoughts. There is a sense of communion now among us.

Working together on this project has been an experience filled with caring and love. We hope that you have found in our stories some of what we have discovered in the process of writing them. We have been inspired, provoked, invigorated—and blessed. We hope you have been as well.

About the Contributors

Earl L. Avery, Ed.D., is Special Assistant to the President of Bentley College for Equal Opportunity. His responsibilities in that position include investigating discrimination and harassment complaints, managing Bentley's diversity project, and cochairing the college's Diversity Steering Committee. On campus, Avery also coteaches a course on managing diversity in the workplace and is actively involved in recruiting and retaining students of color. He is a cofounder of the Minority Scholars Summer Institute in Accountancy program and adviser and liaison to ethnic student organizations such as Bentley's chapter of the National Association of Black Accountants (NABA). Avery received his B.A. from the University of California, Los Angeles, and his master's and Ed.D. degrees in administration, planning, and social policy studies from Harvard University. Previously, Avery was a child advocate who served on the Committee for Special Education for Presidents Johnson and Nixon.

Darlyne Bailey, Ph.D., is Dean and Associate Professor at the Mandel School of Applied Social Sciences at Case Western Reserve University. She has a secondary appointment in the Weatherhead School of Management and chairs the Secretariat of the Mandel Center for Nonprofit Organizations. Bailey draws on her multidisciplinary and polylinguistic approach to life for a constant infusion of creativity and playfulness. Her life's work of discovering and honoring the interconnectedness of all is evident in her publications and research on the development and evaluation of interorganizational collaborations. In this work, Bailey uses participatory action research methodology, partnering herself and students with community members. Her work with Cleveland's Healthy Family/Healthy Start and Hope VI projects have received local and national recognition. Bailey is a Group XIII Fellow in the W. K. Kellogg National Fellowship Program, exploring the role of spirituality in building community.

Myrtle P. Bell is a faculty member at the University of Texas–Arlington, having recently completed her Ph.D. degree in organizational behavior and human resource management. She received her B.B.A. degree in finance from the University of Notre Dame and her M.B.A. from Louisiana State University before beginning a career at IBM Corporation, where she worked in various financial and human resources positions. Her diversity research interests were shaped by growing up in the South during the 1960s and 1970s; being family to numerous international students who found a "home away from home" and taught Bell a great deal about difference and similarity; attending Notre Dame when 99 percent of the population was not Black, 97 percent was not Protestant, and 75 percent was not female; and working at IBM, a fertile diversity learning and teaching ground. Bell's diversity teaching and learning work continues at the University of Texas–Arlington, at home, and in her community.

David M. Boje, Ph.D., is head of the Department of Management at the College of Business Administration and Economics, New Mexico State University. He was formerly Professor of Management at Loyola Marymount University in Los Angeles, where he was director of the Peace Corps Fellows Program and recipient of six Teacher of the Year awards. Boje is editor of the *Journal of Organizational Change Management*, where he accepts mostly qualitative pieces that criticize anything to do with organizations. He has published numerous articles in *Administrative Science Quarterly*, the *Academy of Management Journal*, *Management Science*, and other journals. Boje's main interests are storytelling and deconstruction studies in organizational theory. His most recent book is *Postmodern Management and Organizational Theory*, written with Robert Gephart and Tojo Thatchenkery. His other books include *Managing in the Postmodern World: America's Revolution Against Exploitation* and *Readings in Managerial Psychology*, written with Hal Leavit and Louis Pondy.

Linda McGee Calvert, Ph.D., is interested in change and diversity. She teaches it; she lives it. She taught graduates and undergraduates for eighteen years, did consulting and training work, and held a variety of offices in regional and national organizations. Her writings and presentations were largely focused on women, with change as a central theme. Recently, Calvert completed a clinical psychology internship in the fifth largest school district in the country and continues to learn about diversity. She is grounded by her husband of more than thirty years, her teenage daughter, her octogenarian mother, her two cats, and her backyard filled with raccoons, squirrels, opossums, armadillos, and more than twenty varieties of birds. Fun is science projects, the theater, writing with and visiting her assortment of friends across the country, obtaining another doctorate, and planting fruit trees or wading in the creek on eighty-five acres of gorgeous Texas Hill Country.

Cliff Cheng sees diversity work as honoring differences while finding commonalities so that we may all live in communion. He often sees people using biographical information to stereotype others, cutting off essential dialogue, and assuming permanence in an impermanent world. Cheng considers any piece of biographical detail about himself as past tense and minuscule, an illusion that dissolves the closer one gets.

Dina Comnenou, Ph.D., is Associate Professor at Lesley College in Cambridge, Massachusetts. She is cochair of the Training and Development Committee of Lesley's Diversity Initiative, has developed and directed several graduate degree programs as part of the college's national and international outreach, and teaches graduate-level multidisciplinary courses, including Intercultural Management, Intercultural Issues in the Applied Behavioral Sciences, and Cross-Cultural Transitions. Comnenou is also founder and president of Interculture Inc., an international network of consultants with expertise in organization development, racial and ethnic relations, and intercultural interaction. During her twenty years of consulting, Comnenou has worked nationally and internationally in the public, profit, and nonprofit sectors.

Peter Couch, Ph.D., is a lifelong learner. For fifty years, he has experienced how a White male grows, lives, and works in a world full of support and opportunity. Typical public schooling in Springfield, Illinois, was followed by college, the U.S. Army, a personnel job, graduate work (Ph.D., Wisconsin), and an academic career teaching management. In recent years, new learning and an awakening consciousness of gender and race issues were triggered by his wife's experiences in her own business and by a close working relationship with a female colleague who introduced him to feminist literature and seemed a model of tolerance and understanding. While he still considers himself a novice at "diversity stuff," Couch increasingly attends to diversity issues in his classes and works on being more perceptive about his own lack of awareness and about the subtleties in today's multicultural climate.

Marcy Crary, Ph.D., is Associate Professor of Management at Bentley College in Waltham, Massachusetts. She received her B.A. degree from Harvard and her Ph.D. in organizational behavior from Case Western Reserve University. She is also a graduate of the three-year postgraduate training program at the Gestalt Institute of

Cleveland. Crary's writing, research, and teaching interests concern adult development, the management of diversity in the workplace, and the dynamics of attraction and closeness in work relationships. She helped create Bentley's team-taught course, "Managing Diversity in the Workplace"; is a member of Bentley's Diversity Steering Committee and the Diversity Strategy Group; and works to create faculty development strategies for effectively addressing diversity issues in the classroom. Crary is married, has a stepdaughter and stepson in their twenties, and is the mother of a seven-year-old daughter.

M. Colleen Jones, Ph.D., led a protest to reinstate a popular student athlete to the senior class election ballot and was still recognized by the institution for having done the most for her school. At the University of Iowa, she risked her scholarship to accompany a group to the university president's home at 2:00 A.M. "to make him aware of Black students' concerns" yet completed her studies successfully. At the University of Southern California, Jones discarded the protester garb and enjoyed the beach and the mountains while getting an M.B.A. Despite becoming "a drag on her M.B.A. class's average income," she has enjoyed ten challenging and rewarding years as a college administrator. Returning to school for a doctorate with the intention of obtaining a higher-level administrative position, Jones was bitten by the professorial bug and has been creating memorable learning experiences for herself and her students ever since at George Washington University, Suffolk University, and the University of Nebraska–Lincoln.

Gordon W. Meyer, Ph.D., is Associate Professor of Management at Canisius College in Buffalo, New York. Previously, he taught at Bucknell University. Meyer's experiences with diversity include earning a master's degree at Brigham Young University as a "gentile" (the term applied by members of the Church of Jesus Christ of Latter-Day Saints to those who are not Mormon) and working with rank-and-file members of the United Auto Workers at General Motors Corporation. Meyer is married and the father of an eleven-year-old son. He enjoys the blues, jazz, and exercise.

Lynda L. Moore and *Bonita L. Betters-Reed* have spent nine years together in the Department of Management at Simmons College, where they have coauthored numerous articles, chapters, papers, and presentations. They share a passion for their work on the advancement of women and have taken their "inclusivity for collectivity" message on the road to Barcelona, Montreal, Vancouver, Chicago, and beyond. They are now at work sponsoring a national conference designed to set the agenda for women business owners—in all their diversity—hoping that it will result in the book they have long promised themselves. Moore and Betters-Reed feel fortunate that their friendship has helped them weather personal and professional strains and anticipate their companionship will continue to ease the journey through midlife transitions. Their husbands are good friends, their children humor them, and all get along on joint ski trips, through summer excursions, and at dinner parties. Moore and Betters-Reed look forward to continuing their soulful and humor-filled partnership.

Duncan Spelman, Ph.D., is a bald White guy with a beard who teaches in the Management Department at Bentley College in a suburb of Boston. Spelman also consults to corporations, educational institutions, and nonprofit organizations. The focus and passion of his professional life are diversity, the challenges and opportunities presented by differences in race, gender, sexual orientation, nationality, and other key dimensions of personal identity. The focus and passion of Spelman's personal life are his life partner, Beth; his daughter Elissa; and women's Division II college basketball.

Barbara A. Walker lives, writes, and practices valuing differences in Washington, D.C. She lived there previously when she attended Georgetown Law School and became a civil rights lawyer in the federal government. Shifting from lawyer to advocate, she co-pioneered the development of diversity at Digital Equipment Corporation. She is the first person in the country—maybe the galaxy—to be a Fortune 100 Valuing Differences executive. Walker's writing draws on her work at Digital and in other success-ful—and sometimes not so successful—positions: as vice president for diversity at the University of Cincinnati, a diversity director in California's Silicon Valley, and a diversity and inclusion consultant to an experimental government agency established by presidential initiative. She returned to Washington after a fourteen-year hiatus to deepen relationships with four young grandchildren. Snowbound with them twice in the past two years, she fantasizes about her next career in a climate with no snow.

A Guide to the Contributors' Stories

Part II: Understanding the Diversity Teaching Terrain

Evolution in Definitions of the Work

Choices of Strategies and Arenas for Change

Part III: Distinctive Features of the Landscape

Teacher as Learner

Teacher-Student Relationships and Roles

Future Directions

Name Index

Subject Index

A

Academy of Management, Women in Management Division of, 11, 84, 97

African Americans: and identity, 4–9, 26–27, 33; "othered" experiences of, 46–47

Aid to Families with Dependent Children (AFDC), 168

AIDS shelter project, 124

American Assembly of Collegiate Schools of Business, 81

Anger, for educators, 167–171

Antioch University, identity at, 11

B

Baton Rouge: false arrest in, 9; teaching through *being* in, 151–152

Being: diversity as, 43–44, 45–46, 213–214; space for, 95–96; in Tao, 203; teaching through, 151–153

Belles, 162

Bentley College: identity at, 5, 22–24; preparation at, 38–39, 42; team teaching at, 145–149

Black Student Union, 162

Boston College, identity at, 13

Brigham Young University: identity at, 28, 153–154; "othered" experience at, 48–49; preparation at, 40

Bucknell University: identity at, 29; leaving, 161; teacher as learner at, 109–110

C

California, multicultural materials in, 4

California at Los Angeles, University of (UCLA), mentor at, 36

China, *quanxi* concept in 96

Chinese American: and identity, 18–19; joy of being, 194–195

Church of Jesus Christ of Latter-Day Saints, (LDS), 48–49, 154

Collaborative learning: in diversity teaching, 76; identity from, 9–15

Collegiate Press, 163

Commitment: social, 202–203; sustaining, 181–185

Community: by diversity educators, 187–190; importance of, 222–224

Cornell University, identity at, 29

Creativity, 182

Culture shock, 94–95

D

Daimon concept, 41

Developmental stages, and paradox, 219

POINT LOMA NAZARENE UNIVERSITY RYAN LIBRARY